The Mark of
Zion

The Mark of Zion

Congregational Life in Black Churches

Stephen C. Rasor and
Michael I. N. Dash

Foreword by Carl S. Dudley

THE
PILGRIM
PRESS
Cleveland

To

Charles Edgar Rasor and Lydia Lee Rasor
and to the memory of
Eleanor Marie Rasor Appman
and to
Donald Josiah and Shirley Eloise Dash,
William Clark and Eugenia Porter Turner,
Ancestors in the cloud of witnesses
in the Church Triumphant

The Pilgrim Press
700 Prospect Avenue
Cleveland, Ohio 44115-1100
pilgrimpress.com

© 2003 by Stephen C. Rasor and Michael I. N. Dash

All rights reserved. Published 2003

Printed in the United States of America on acid-free paper

08   07   06   05   04   03   5   4   3   2   1

Library of Congress Cataloging-in-Publication Data
Rasor, Stephen Charles.
   The mark of Zion : congregational life in Black churches / Stephen C.
Rasor and Michael I. N. Dash.
      p.   cm.
   Companion book to: The shape of Zion.
   Includes bibliographical references (p.   ) and index.
   ISBN 0-8298-1576-7 (pbk. : alk. paper)
   1. African Americans – Religion.   I. Dash, Michael I. N.   II. Title.
BR563.N4R33   2003
277.3′083′08996073 – dc22

                                                          2003062326

CONTENTS

FOREWORD

This book announces a new chapter in the remarkable history of the Interdenominational Theological Center in Atlanta as the premier information center and resource for understanding the Black Church experience in America. For half a century the ITC has shaped the leaders of that most vibrant and resilient faith tradition, the historic Black churches. In this collaborative institution the candidates for leadership are mentored into powerful messengers who combine dynamic worship and spellbinding preaching with unrivaled dedication to evangelical outreach and social justice.

The historic genius of the ITC is expressed in the beliefs and religious practices woven from six proud and distinct denominational sources that maintain their separate integrity even as they draw from their common Black Church tradition. The ITC provides a contemporary framework for a religious rainbow of Black churches, historic, pentecostal, and mainline, including African Methodist Episcopal (Turner Theological Seminary), Baptist (Morehouse School of Religion), Church of God in Christ (Charles H. Mason Theological Seminary), Christian Methodist Episcopal (Phillips School of Theology), Presbyterian Church (U.S.A.) (Johnson C. Smith Theological Seminary), and United Methodist (Gammon Theological Seminary). In diversity they are united.

In this book we witness the beginning of a new phase in the ITC as it establishes itself as a national resource for research data and interpretation of the Black Church experience. As an academic institution, the ITC has always been unusually involved in the practice of ministry. Typically the women and men of its student body fill leadership positions in churches and other ministries throughout the region. Into the classrooms they bring their genuine concerns from their life situations, challenging professors to help them shape faith on the anvil of problems faced by real people in many different institutions. These students seek an understanding of Christian faith that makes a difference — a biblical, systematic, and genuinely practical theology.

Research in the ITC must be equally God-centered and earth-bound. It must speak to people in the trenches at the front lines of Christian faith. Data must be practical in consequences and useful to strengthen the vitality of congregations. Analysis without payoff seems irrelevant to working church leaders. Theory and theology must frame the issues in ways that help overcome barriers and move people into action. Academics must make sense where poverty of body and spirit cries out for active engagement toward the fullness of God's grace and powers for healing.

Authors Stephen Rasor and Michael Dash of the ITC faculty are uniquely prepared and positioned to respond to such a challenge. Grounded in practical wisdom from their years of personal experience, scholarly research, and oversight of ministerial students, they have given us a truly unique and eminently useful report on African American congregational life at the new millennium.

They understand that data need contexts, both where it came from and why it is important. They recognize that research must tackle hard issues of ministry. Although they treat the Black Church tradition with great respect, they are not afraid to raise questions and push the past to engage the future. As educators they know that pain contributes to learning, and criticism is essential for growth. As seminary leaders, they recognize that the core purpose of theory is to integrate material, and that of theology is to give it depth and meaning.

Dash and Rasor start with a singular and significant asset. They love the Church — not uncritically, but as leaders who have been nurtured in communities of caring believers. In a previous publication, *Hidden Wholeness: An African American Spirituality for Individuals and Congregations* (Pilgrim, 1997), they examined the communal and cultural spiritual dynamics that have theological roots with very practical expressions for pastors and church members. Therefore they wrote from a reservoir of personal and professional experience; in this new publication they have assembled reports from hundreds of congregations to confirm and expand their observations.

Through their leadership, the Interdenominational Theological Center participated in Faith Communities Today (FACT), the largest survey of congregations ever conducted in the United States. FACT data includes information from 14,301 congregations in 41 denominations and faith groups, which together represent about 90 percent of worshipers in the United States. These denominations and faith groups worked cooperatively in 26 separate studies and joined the common project organized by the Hartford Institute for Religion Research, with funding provided jointly by the Lilly Endowment and each of the participating groups.

Rasor and Dash record the views of leaders in 1,863 congregations in the Black Church tradition. Here for the first time we can see the similarities between Black churches and other major religious movements throughout the nation. We see the obvious elements analyzed (like worship and community witness), and we see the hidden dimensions revealed (like financial challenges and leadership struggles). In this profile we also see the bold uniqueness of the Black Church tradition, its energy and tenacity across generations and throughout America.

The authors have created remarkable portraits in paradoxical tension. They show the diversity of religious practices and beliefs in each of the denominations, that is, the distinctive character of Baptists, Presbyterians, Methodists, and Pentecostals. But at the same time they demonstrate in bold relief *E Pluribus Unum,* the unity within diversity of the shared Black Church tradition, found so desirable in the earlier work of C. Eric Lincoln and Lawrence H. Mamiya, *The Black Church in the African American Experience* (Duke University Press, 1990). Rasor and Dash let these data show us how these traditions are different, and yet how they are the same.

Lawrence H. Mamiya was also a moving force in making this study possible. From his own professional contributions, he brought to the project a stature and an active base of information and experience that greatly expands the value of the study. Through the collaboration of Mamiya and the seminary leaders, the Interdenominational Theological Center has now become the largest and most significant source of solid historical and current information on the Black Church experience in America, unrivaled throughout the world. The ITC is the natural home for such a treasury of reliable observations, experiences, and interpretations. The book marks an invitation for all who are interested to share in data that interpret, critique, and champion the unique strength of the Black Church tradition.

Stephen Rasor and Michael Dash have given but a glimpse of the wealth of the Black churches, warmly presented with anecdotes and inspiration. This is a wonderful beginning, and we look forward to an engaging conversation with much more to come.

CARL S. DUDLEY
Hartford Institute for Religion Research
Hartford Seminary, Hartford, Connecticut

ACKNOWLEDGMENTS

We are grateful to many persons in our ITC community who have provided support services in a variety of ways as we have engaged in this project. Special thanks are due to Reta Bigham, Cecelia Dixon, Melody Berry, and Janette King.

We express deep gratitude and appreciation to all our colleagues at the Interdenominational Theological Center, especially those who have been our conversation partners: Christine Chapman, Edward Smith, and Marsha Snulligan Haney, our fellows in the Institute for Black Religious Life (IBRL). In both formal and incidental encounters, we benefited from their scholarship. We appreciate the enthusiastic support, knowledge, and wisdom of all our colleagues. They also shared with us their varied experiences and a passion for congregations and persons who seek deeper relationship with God in those faith communities. We also honor the memory of the late Jonathan Jackson, colleague and friend, who collaborated with us on a previous writing project, generous in his wisdom and knowledge and gracious in his affirmation and support.

We greatly appreciate the support of our six denominational deans in this endeavor: Thomas Brown, Oliver Haney, Daniel Jacobs, Walter McKelvey, William Perkins, and David Wallace. They actively participated in our research project, ITC Project 2000 and made it possible to complete this detailed process.

The overwhelming majority of the data gathering and the initial interpretation of that data was done in cooperation with the

Gallup Organization. However, we also want to thank Adair Lummis of the Hartford Seminary for her assistance in the analysis of some of the data.

We are indebted to Carl Dudley and Lawrence Mamiya, who gave us the opportunity to participate in the project on the survey of religious life in the United States in 2000. The results of that research are documented in *Faith Communities Today: A Report on Religion in the United States Today*. This book offers interpretation of data gathered on the historically Black denominations. We would also mention L. Kay Pendleton and Da Vita McCallister, who listened to our ideas and offered thoughtful insights and suggestions. We, however, assume ultimate responsibility for the perspectives we have presented in this book.

In the course of our work, we have visited many congregations and worked with them and their pastors. Although we do not identify specific congregations, the narratives we have shared in this book reflect the aspects of congregational life we have observed. We are grateful for the generous sharing of those pastors and leaders. We salute the tireless and devoted service that they render as they lead their congregations to faithful and obedient ministry in church and world.

Finally, each of us is grateful to members of our immediate families. We could not have persevered without their unwavering love, support and encouragement. This book is a small offering to Susan and Joshua; and to Linda, Jan, Ginneh, Richard, Michelle, and Nathaniel for their love, patience, respect, and selfless support.

INTRODUCTION

Anyone with any degree of sensitivity knows that things are not right with our world. The events of September 11, 2001, were a magnified example, as are the ongoing struggles in the Middle East. Misdirected fanatics of one religion fight and kill others devoted to another. Impoverished people and nations valued less by Western countries continue in the cycle of oppression and dehumanization. AIDS rages throughout the world; it has been estimated that the epidemic will claim 68 million lives by 2020. This is roughly the number of people killed in all the wars of the twentieth century combined. In Africa and in the United States this killer disease is eliminating people of color in significantly disproportionate numbers. Economic injustice, whether in the collapse of a large corporation or the moving of a manufacturing plant to a two-thirds world setting, impacts millions of people. Things are not right with the human family.

In our book *Hidden Wholeness: An African American Spirituality for Individuals and Communities,* we argued that "the world appears to be void of any universal religious meaning, certainly not an embracing spiritual wholeness."[1] We suggested that a hidden wholeness or deeper spirituality that connects individuals and communities was often absent. However, one of the important manifestations of that hidden wholeness was in the faith communities of our society. Our churches, synagogues, and masjids function as mediating structures between and among individuals and the larger society. Not always, but often, these religious communities

1

help individuals, families, and local communities transcend some of our worst social realities. Our bodies of faith help people discover a deeper spirituality that opens them to a God who can "make a way out of no way." In the face of racism, sexism, and economic injustice many of our religious communities have chosen to follow God as God has acted on behalf of God's people.

Fundamentally we believe that God has the world in God's hand. The events of September 11, 2001, and many such events before and after that day might suggest for some that God's hand has slipped. Some would argue that God has turned away from God's people. If we allow ourselves to see the world and its many horrific realities in limited ways, this is a natural conclusion to draw. If there is no understanding of and commitment to a Supreme Being who created the human family, one who acts continuously on its behalf and redeems human existence even in the midst of tragic human and societal failure, then God talk in the present is absurd. But we do not believe that God talk, and particularly spirituality, is in any way absurd. We have been nurtured by our faith communities and have been blessed by significant others who have taught us a more hopeful way.

We come from and reside in the Christian community. We have learned from and value other religious expressions and contexts. We practice ministry in a Protestant interdenominational setting. The majority of our colleagues and students are African American men and women who teach us daily about our collective journey. We have been blessed on our journey; we celebrate that in part by writing this book.

Recently we concluded a major study of Black congregational life. We examined the historically Black denominations, including Black United Methodist and Black Presbyterian (U.S.A.) churches. Our exploration of Black congregational life was conducted within the context of a larger national project, Faith Communities Today

(FACT). Carl S. Dudley and David A. Roozen of the Hartford Institute for Religion Research directed this major national project. FACT is the largest survey of congregations ever administered in the United States. It appears to be the most inclusive denominationally sanctioned program of interfaith cooperation.

Our ITC/FaithFactor Project 2000 Study of Black churches was a significant component of the FACT study, a research endeavor that revealed many significant and vital realities of America's religious landscape. The data collected as a part of Project 2000 informs this book. The data from the FACT study is currently the most comprehensive and accurate information available on the character and culture of Black congregational life. This book tells part of the story of African American religiosity in the year 2000. Our hope is that it will enable local pastors, seminary students, denominational officials, and others to understand better what Black churches are doing regarding worship, spiritual growth, community outreach, managing, and leading.

More importantly, the FACT study and our own research on African American religious life reveal some exciting news about religiosity in the United States. Our faith communities are strong and vital. While we are significantly diverse and at points quite unique, we share many things in common. As Roman Catholics, Protestants, Jews, and Muslims we believe and act on our beliefs in different ways. But overall our study of religion in the United States at the turn of the century celebrates the many and lasting influences of current congregational life. Our faith communities are sources of unity and cohesion. They are an important heritage, providing clarity of purpose, moral grounding, and sources of meaning for people's lives. Many of our religious bodies are growing and thereby incorporating individuals and families into their common life. Our faith communities provide corporate worship and activities for growth. Diverse religious bodies are constantly offering community outreach, social programs, and projects that address many of our societal problems.

Religion in America is vital and alive. It is helping men and women, boys and girls, to experience life at a more comprehensive level. The hidden wholeness we discussed in our previous text (1997) can be measured in part in the orthodoxy and orthopraxy of our faith groupings — in the intellectual assent to prescribed religious doctrines and to the proper performance of religious duties or rituals. We are not all the same. We will never believe and practice our faith in an identical fashion. But we appear to be similar in some very important ways. Our faith groups function as mediating structures in our society in ways that help people collectively and personally not only survive but flourish. Our churches, synagogues, and masjids are making major contributions to the welfare of persons where they are located. Through many efforts spirituality and social support are blended. Bodies of faith nurture people and communities.

Many people in the world experience, at differing levels, seemingly unbearable hardships related to health, food, and shelter. Many are victimized by U.S. foreign policies both directly and indirectly. Individuals and ethnic groups in this country daily face dehumanizing and oppressive realities. And yet our faith groups, acting in and beyond congregational life, are making a difference. They refuse to be rebuffed by racism, sexism, and economic injustice.

There is good news in America's religious landscape. God has not abandoned God's people. God has been active in our lives and continues to be committed to being God for and with us. Our discernment of God and God's faith communities is hopeful. With our experience in the Church, in a seminary setting, within our families and in our spiritual journeys, we claim God's affirmation and love. God has called us and other men and women in pastoral leadership roles to be obedient and faithful. We bring to our task a deep and earnest commitment.

Our particular research interest produced an examination of approximately nineteen hundred African American churches across this country — rural, urban, and suburban. The Gallup Organization assisted in this project, interviewing pastors and senior lay leaders of Black and predominantly Black congregations in the spring of 2000. Our initial findings were published in seven documents we developed along with Christine D. Chapman (2001).[2] These seven documents presented our overall analysis of the following Black denominations: Baptist, Church of God in Christ, African Methodist Episcopal, Christian Methodist Episcopal, African Methodist Episcopal Zion, Black United Methodist, and Black Presbyterian (U.S.A.). This book will tell the larger story. (See the appendix for the research methods used in this study.)

It is an important story to tell. The African American Church in the United States takes its place alongside the other faith communities of our land. Like others, it has learned how to be a context for healing and transformation. The Black Church presents a vital model for faithfulness in word and deed. African American congregations have their problems, as is the case for other faith groups. But they also have assets. They have strengths, practices, and promises.

In the following chapters we share with you some general demographic facts about this special faith community. We paint a picture of their self-understanding. We focus on worship, one of the most important and essential aspects of religious community life. We reveal the activities of the members inside the churches as well as their serious attempt to reach beyond their doors. We explore the varied and rich set of resources that exist within the Black religious setting. Finally we share our ideas concerning leadership and its ever-expanding characteristics.

We are aware that what we have to present has different meanings for readers of this book. Some are pastors of local churches. Others are preparing for ministry, while still others are engaged in preparing men and women for service in and beyond the local congregation. To take seriously the various interests, we explore African American congregational life from four perspectives. First, we provide a profile of Black congregational life from a national perspective. Then we make this more specific as we give an example of a local church setting that illustrates some aspect of that national profile. Third, we assist you in considering the applicability of this profile and local example to your experience. Finally, we invite you to consider future ministry in the light of these findings and the challenges that arise from this exploration. In a word we look at the *facts* (national profile), explore some of the *faces* (local congregations), consider the *feelings* that you have in regard to this information, and finally offer options for the *future* as we engage in our respective ministries. We also include some biblical-theological reflections on the faith journey and the practice of ministry. It is our desire to make this picture of Black congregational life as transparent as possible. We believe that the facts, faces, feelings, and future are all part of the same landscape. But it is a picture that has been drawn in a multiplicity of ways and one that is discerned in various ways as well. Whether you are a pastor, student, or professor, we hope the picture we have drawn will be appreciated and redrawn in your life and ministry.

We celebrate the fact that God continues to participate in our collective life, especially congregational life. Black congregational life is vigorous and alive. We want to share that reality with you.

1

BLACK CHURCHES

AN OVERVIEW

We visited Hillcrest, where the Rev. Stephanie Madison, the assistant pastor, led the Invitation to Discipleship, the Offering (this was a marching ritual), and Community Concerns (which gave the impression that this was a full-service congregation). We learned that there were 24 different ministries and 800 active members, with 120 regularly participating. Birthdays and wedding anniversaries were recognized. The sixteen-page bulletin provides a wealth of information about the life and activities at Hillcrest: last week's attendance; "...Remember to pray for...who are sick or shut in"; a tithes chart (so one can compute one's giving); the activities and ministries of the church during the week; events to come. In the foyer there is other literature, including leaflets in profusion.

In informal conversation with some members during the fellowship hour after worship, they said that worship is something that their congregation does very well. As they understood it, worship included "giving God glory," "helping others by giving hope," prayer, praise, "giving time to God," etc. Everyone in the group agreed that worship is transformation. As one of the members expressed it, "It was as if your soul, with all its impurities gathered

---

*Throughout the book we provide vignettes of typical congregational situations. The names have been changed, but the situations described are real.

through the traffic of life during the week, were open to the cleansing, healing, and renewing of the Spirit of God through the worship. Then as you move out from the sanctuary, you are re-created and refreshed for the ongoing life journey, a new person."

As a worshiping community, Hillcrest included public testimonials concerning the goodness of God and the desire to share the worship experience with people outside the church community. The worship experience was one part of the rhythm of the Christian life; the other was engagement in the world beyond the sanctuary doors, joining God in the work that God was already doing in the world.

Our study of African American congregations has given us a greater appreciation of the "Black sacred cosmos" described by C. Eric Lincoln and Lawrence H. Mamiya. The African American church has at its center an important sacred component.

> The Black sacred cosmos or the religious worldview of African Americans is related both to their African heritage, which envisaged the whole universe as sacred, and to their conversion to Christianity during slavery and its aftermath. It has been only in the past twenty years that scholars of African American history, culture, and religion have begun to recognize that Black people created their own unique and distinctive form of culture and worldviews as parallels rather than replication of the culture in which they were involuntary guests.[3]

Black Churches in the United States

Over half (52 percent) of the Black churches in the total sample are located in the South (Fig. 1.1). Nearly one-quarter (24 percent) are located in the north central part of the United States, while smaller

Figure 1.1. Total Sample of Black Churches: Location by Region of the United States

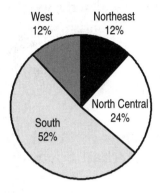

West 12% Northeast 12%

North Central 24%

South 52%

Figure 1.2. Black Denominational Groups: Location by Region of the United States

	Northeast	North Central	South	West
Baptist	9%	28%	52%	11%
COGIC	11%	28%	39%	22%
AME	18%	23%	49%	10%
CME	5%	14%	75%	6%
AMEZ	37%	17%	42%	4%
UMC	10%	20%	68%	2%
Presbyterian	18%	19%	56%	7%

percentages are found in the Northeast (12 percent) and West (12 percent).

This southern grounding of the Black Church can be seen more clearly in some of the individual African American denominations (Fig. 1.2). The Christian Methodist Episcopal denomination (with 75 percent of its membership in the South), Black United Methodists (68 percent), Black Presbyterians (U.S.A.) (56 percent), and the Baptists (52 percent) are predominantly located in the southern part of the United States. Other churches, like African Methodist

Episcopal Zion, are not as strong in the South (42 percent), But their presence in the Northeast is evident (37 percent). Relatively few Black churches are located in the western part of this country. Only the Church of God in Christ (with 22 percent in the West) has had significant expansion in that region. Black United Methodist denominational churches (2 percent) are almost nonexistent in the West.

Black Churches in Rural, Suburban, and Urban Locations

The Black Church is a southern institution; it is also an urban one (Fig. 1.3). Most of the African American congregations (66 percent) are located in urban areas. Black churches in suburban communities represent less than one-quarter of the total sample (22 percent), while rural settings (12 percent) have still fewer Black congregations.

Baptists are numerous in the city (with 79 percent of Baptist congregations in urban settings), but much less so in the rural areas (5 percent, Fig. 1.4). Many African Methodist Episcopal Zion churches are found in suburbia (32 percent), while Black

Figure 1.3. Total Sample of Black Churches:
Location by Community Surrounding the Church

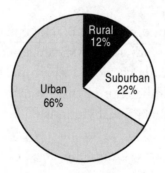

Figure 1.4. Black Denominational Groups:
Location by Community Surrounding the Church

	Rural	Suburban	Urban
Baptist	5%	16%	79%
COGIC	11%	25%	64%
AME	15%	22%	63%
CME	28%	23%	49%
AMEZ	14%	32%	54%
UMC	4%	21%	75%
Presbyterian	11%	14%	75%

Presbyterian (U.S.A.) churches (14 percent) are less visible in that location. Rural Christian Methodist Episcopal churches (28 percent) are more evident than Black United Methodist churches (4 percent). These findings illustrate that while the African American Church is mostly a southern, urban phenomenon, there are significant variations among the different groups. These churches serve different people across the country in all its variations — rural, suburban, and urban.

When considering the locations of Black churches with one hundred or more active adult members things change somewhat (Fig. 1.5). These churches are more likely to be found in cities

Figure 1.5. Black Churches with 100+ Active Members:
Percentage by Location

	Rural	Suburban	Urban
Total Sample	23%	46%	53%
Baptist	44%	68%	81%
COGIC	12%	31%	30%
AME	47%	60%	65%
CME	8%	24%	42%
AMEZ	33%	36%	46%
UMC	33%	74%	66%
Presbyterian	27%	23%	49%

(where 53 percent have one hundred or more members) and suburban areas (46 percent) than in small towns and rural areas
(23 percent). This distribution varies even more when we examine individual denominational groups. Denominations with large
urban churches are the Baptists (with 81 percent of the urban
churches having a hundred or more active members), Black United
Methodist (66 percent), and African Methodist Episcopal (65 percent). Among the rural Black churches, those with somewhat
larger memberships are the African Methodist Episcopal (with 47
percent of the rural churches having a hundred or more active
members) and Baptist (44 percent).

Size of Black Churches

Over half (53 percent) of the churches in the total sample of
Black churches have fewer than one hundred regularly participating adult members (Fig. 1.6). Interestingly, 28 percent have fewer
than fifty active adult members. Church of God in Christ churches
have many small membership churches (46 percent) with less than
fifty regularly participating congregants. Black United Methodist Church congregations (53 percent), Baptist (48 percent), and
African Methodist Episcopal (45 percent) have higher percentages
of churches with 100–349 active members. Black religiosity varies
by location, region, and size. They are not all the same and thus
offer different gifts to their respective communities.

Year Congregations Were Organized

Over half (57 percent) of the churches in the total sample of Black
churches were organized before 1945 (Fig. 1.7). Almost all the
individual denominational groups organized a majority of their
churches before 1945. The Church of God in Christ, however,

Figure 1.6. Size of Black Churches by Denomination

	Under 50	50–99	100–349	350+
Total	28%	25%	36%	11%
Baptist	11%	20%	48%	21%
COGIC	46%	27%	22%	5%
AME	16%	23%	45%	16%
CME	28%	25%	36%	11%
AMEZ	25%	33%	37%	5%
UMC	13%	21%	53%	13%
Presbyterian	24%	34%	39%	3%

Figure 1.7. Black Congregations by Year Organized

	Before 1945	1945–1965	1966–1989	1990–2000
Total	57%	20%	18%	5%
Baptist	50%	25%	21%	4%
COGIC	24%	27%	38%	11%
AME	88%	9%	2%	1%
CME	82%	9%	5%	4%
AMEZ	79%	11%	5%	5%
UMC	74%	15%	9%	2%
Presbyterian	70%	22%	5%	3%

organized almost half (49 percent) of their congregations since 1966. Most of the Black denominations have not organized many churches in the 1990–2000 period, e.g. (with only 1 percent of their churches organized in that period), Black United Methodist (2 percent), and Black Presbyterian (U.S.A.) (3 percent). These findings suggest implications for church growth patterns and will be discussed later in this chapter.

Black Churches Begun after 1965

Black churches organized after 1965 are more likely to be in the western part of the United States than in other regions (Fig. 1.8).

**Figure 1.8. Black Churches Established after 1965
by Percentage of Churches in Each Region**

	Northeast	South	North Central	West
Total	22%	19%	26%	40%
Baptist	35%	21%	24%	39%
COGIC	52%	49%	45%	53%
AME	0%	3%	2%	8%
CME	8%	7%	17%	7%
AMEZ	8%	2%	18%	75%
UMC	0%	10%	17%	50%
Presbyterian	0%	9%	6%	29%

This recent westward expansion in members includes the Baptist denomination (with 39 percent of the churches in the West organized since 1965). However, proportionately more Baptist congregations were organized after 1965 in the Northeast than in the total sample of Black churches. Church of God in Christ congregations have expanded in all areas of the country. The recent western expansion includes the African Methodist Episcopal Zion (75 percent), Black United Methodist (50 percent), and Black Presbyterian (U.S.A.) (29 percent) denominations but not the Christian Methodist Episcopal, which has a greater proportion of recently established churches in the north central area of the United States.

Membership Changes since 1996

About three-fifths (58 percent) of the African American parishes in the United States experienced at least a 5 percent increase in membership during the period 1996–2000 (Fig. 1.9). This is true for all seven of the denominations analyzed in this study. Only a small minority of Black churches among the seven denominational

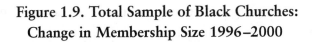

Figure 1.9. Total Sample of Black Churches: Change in Membership Size 1996–2000

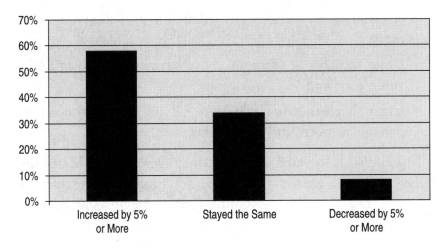

Figure 1.10. Increase in Membership since 1996 among Churches That Have Experienced Growth, by Size of Congregation

Number of Active Adults	Percentage Increase in Membership
50 or fewer	46%
50–99	56%
100–149	59%
150–349	70%
350–999	73%
1000 or more	81%

groups (8 percent) experienced a 5 percent or more decrease in membership.

Churches with a membership of fifty to ninety-nine experienced 56 percent growth in the last five years (Fig. 1.10). Churches with one thousand or more active adults experienced an 81 percent growth. The larger the membership, the more likely a 5 percent or more growth occurred during the five year period. The reasons for this include the following:

- larger churches are typically situated in growing population areas;
- larger churches are more likely to have additional staff and volunteers; and
- larger churches have a wider diversity of programs to engage present members and attract new members.

It was also discovered, however, that even in churches of different sizes, the greater the number of programs presented to members, the more likely the church grew in membership between 1996 and 2000.

Summary and Conclusion

Generally speaking what have we learned so far about Black congregational life at the turn of the century? The African American Church is located in the South and in the north central part of the United States. It is a city church for the most part. A majority of the Black churches have fewer than a hundred regularly participating adult members. Half of the churches in this sample of Black congregations were organized before 1945. Very few African American parishes came into existence in the period 1990–2000.

Recent establishment of Black churches has taken place especially in the western part of the United States. Most African American churches have experienced some level of growth in recent times. Larger churches and churches with more programs for their members and others are the churches that are growing. Now we turn to the members themselves.

2

PARISHIONERS IN BLACK CONGREGATIONS

We had requested conversation with anyone who was available, and they were waiting for us, the visitors. You could have described them as smart young Black professionals. One of them, Lucinda, discovered that Alicia, like her, worked for Ford Motor Company in Detroit — "Motown." They were involved in designing prototypes of new automobiles. Much of the conversation turned around that and their eager anticipation of what the products would look like.

Lucinda and Alicia were just two among a significant group of young adults in that congregation, educated, intelligent, and invested in the church. The young people spoke up and spoke out. "We are a large church, but we are working at making it feel like a family. There is every attempt and invitation to be involved, and an assurance given that there is some place that you can minister and use your gifts. Persons are encouraged to discern their gifts." One person stated that she discerned that her gift was the ability to diffuse tensions. When she used this gift, she was allowed to grow. She understood that sometimes gifts are discerned experientially.

Also in that group was Linda, chair of evangelism and mission outreach. She had been a member for twenty-eight years and was considered one of the matriarchs of the congregation. Charles was a teacher of one of the Bible study groups and was also one of the

Figure 2.1. Total Sample of Black Churches:
Characteristics of Active Members

Commute 15+ minutes	24%
New members	5%
Family income below $20K	9%
Ages 18–35	9%
Age over 60	7%
College graduates	14%

elders in the church, having been a member for over twenty years. Then there was Donald, chairperson of the Men's Group. He also organized work on the buildings and grounds and enhanced the music ministry with his trumpet. Each of these persons discovered in their church a place where they belonged, where they were affirmed in their person and permitted to share their knowledge, gifts, and faith with others who sought through their lives to bring the reign of God nearer in everyday life.

To begin to comprehend Black religious life one has to understand the makeup of its congregational membership. Actively participating adults have certain characteristics that suggest in some ways who they are and what they are like (Fig. 2.1). If we look at the total sample of active members among African American churches nationwide, we see that nearly one-quarter of these commute more than fifteen minutes to attend their local churches. Pastors estimate that overall only 5 percent of new persons who join are not being assimilated into their respective fellowships. Family income is another important characteristic. In this study 9 percent of the active membership had a family income of less than $20,000. Attracting and maintaining young adults is important to church growth. In this project 9 percent of the active participants are in the eighteen- to thirty-five-year-old age range. The aging of membership in congregations is also a significant concern in the local church. On average 7 percent of the active

Figure 2.2. Black Denominational Groups:
Characteristics of Active Members

	Commute 15+ Minutes	New Members	Family Income below $20K	Ages 18–35	Age 60+	College Graduates
Total	24%	5%	9%	9%	7%	14%
Baptist	22%	5%	6%	9%	5%	10%
COGIC	25%	6%	12%	12%	3%	5%
AME	24%	5%	7%	8%	9%	20%
CME	24%	5%	15%	9%	9%	16%
AMEZ	25%	6%	9%	5%	10%	21%
UMC	26%	2%	4%	5%	14%	28%
Presbyterian	26%	1%	3%	7%	9%	40%

members of Black churches are over the age of sixty. Finally, the number of college graduates (14 percent) is another revealing characteristic in Black religiosity.

Again there is variation among the individual denominational groups as compared to the total sample of African American congregations (Fig. 2.2). Baptist congregational participants reflect demographic characteristics similar to the total sample, although with Baptist congregations there is some variation from the overall average in household income and college graduates. Baptist churches have fewer active members with family income below $20,000 (6 percent) than the total sample (9 percent). The total sample shows more college graduates (14 percent) than do the Baptists (10 percent).

Church of God in Christ congregational participants reflect demographic characteristics similar to the total sample of Black churches, although there are slight variances from the total sample. Church of God in Christ churches have more active family members (12 percent) whose income falls below $20,000 than do Black churches generally (9 percent). Black parishes overall (9 percent) claimed fewer younger people (eighteen to thirty-five years old) than the Church of God in Christ congregations (12 percent).

Church of God in Christ churches also have fewer older members (3 percent) than the total sample of churches (7 percent). And college graduates are fewer (5 percent) than in the Black churches in general (14 percent).

African Methodist Episcopal congregational participants also reflect demographic characteristics similar to the total sample of Black churches. African Methodist Episcopal churches, however, account for few families (7 percent) with income below $20,000 as compared to African American parishes overall. African Methodist Episcopal denominational groups have more older active members (9 percent) than the total Black Church sample (7 percent). In addition African Methodist Episcopal religious communities claim more college graduates (20 percent) than was found among the total group of churches (14 percent).

Christian Methodist Episcopal congregational participants reflect demographic characteristics similar to the total sample of Black churches. However, Christian Methodist Episcopal congregations show a slight variance from the overall sample in families below $20,000 in annual income, congregants over sixty years of age, and college graduates. Christian Methodist Episcopal churches seem to attract more families with lower incomes (15 percent) than do Black churches generally (9 percent). They have more adults who are older (9 percent) and more college graduates (16 percent) than the total sample of Black congregations.

African Methodist Episcopal Zion congregational participants likewise reflect demographic characteristics similar to the total sample of Black churches. However, with African Methodist Episcopal Zion congregations there is some variance in younger active members, older members, and college graduates. African Methodist Episcopal Zion churches have more persons over sixty years of age (10 percent) and fewer young people (5 percent) than Black churches overall. African Methodist Episcopal Zion churches have significantly more college graduates (21 percent) than the total sample of Black parishes (14 percent).

Black United Methodist Church congregational participants reflect demographic characteristics similar to the total sample of Black churches only in the category of time to commute. United Methodist Church faith communities claim fewer new members (2 percent) than do Black churches nationwide (5 percent). They have fewer active families with income below $20,000 (4 percent) than was seen among all Black churches (9 percent). The UMC congregations have fewer young people (5 percent) and more members who are older (14 percent) than the total sample, and they have attracted more college graduates (28 percent) than the Black Church in general (14 percent).

Black Presbyterian (U.S.A.) congregational participants reflect demographic characteristics similar to the total sample of Black churches. However, Black parishes generally claim higher percentages of new members (5 percent) than do the Black Presbyterian churches (1 percent). Fewer younger adults (7 percent) and more older adults (9 percent) make up Presbyterian (U.S.A.) churches than is the case with the overall sample. Additionally, the number of college graduates among Black Presbyterian (U.S.A.) churches (40 percent) is significantly higher than among Black churches in general (14 percent).

Finally, when the seven denominational groups are compared among themselves, certain characteristics surface. All denominational bodies have significant percentages of active members who commute fifteen minutes or more to their churches. Most denominational entities are attracting new people, but two groups are doing so less often — United Methodist and Presbyterian (U.S.A.). Christian Methodist Episcopal (15 percent) and Church of God in Christ (12 percent) denominations are attracting families with lower incomes than is the case among the other denominational groups. United Methodist (4 percent) and Presbyterian (U.S.A.) (3 percent) churches have fewer families with income below $20,000. Church of God in Christ congregations (12 percent) have more young people proportionally than the others. United Methodist (14 percent) and African Methodist Episcopal Zion (10 percent) claim higher percentages of persons over sixty years of age. Presbyterian (U.S.A.) (40 percent), United Methodist (28 percent), African Methodist Episcopal Zion (21 percent), African Methodist Episcopal (20 percent), and Christian Methodist Episcopal (16 percent) are attracting college graduates; Church of God in Christ (5 percent) and Baptist churches (10 percent) are doing so less often.

Location

Among the three locations — rural, urban, and suburban — there is no significant difference in the presence of college graduates among Baptist church members (Fig. 2.3). Urban churches have slightly higher percentages of persons between eighteen and thirty-five and over sixty years of age. Persons in urban and suburban areas are more likely to commute over fifteen minutes to church compared to those in rural areas.

There are slight differences in all categories among Church of God in Christ members. A higher percentage in urban areas is more likely to commute to church over fifteen minutes and to have greater numbers of congregants between eighteen and thirty-five.

There is a significant difference in the presence of college graduates in urban areas among the African Methodist Episcopal churches. A higher percentage of persons attending AME churches in suburban and urban areas is also more likely to commute over fifteen minutes to church as compared to the percentage in rural

Figure 2.3. Characteristics of Black Denominational Groups
by Location

	College Graduates	Age 60+	Ages 18–35	New Members	Commute 15+ Mins.
Baptist					
Rural	35%	15%	31%	15%	27%
Urban	35%	25%	39%	22%	57%
Suburban	30%	16%	34%	21%	51%
COGIC					
Rural	10%	10%	27%	17%	37%
Urban	21%	12%	41%	19%	52%
Suburban	21%	15%	31%	21%	42%
AME					
Rural	38%	34%	43%	35%	24%
Urban	50%	34%	34%	15%	57%
Suburban	34%	36%	18%	12%	48%
CME					
Rural	33%	34%	25%	14%	33%
Urban	37%	31%	28%	16%	62%
Suburban	29%	22%	20%	16%	36%
AMEZ					
Rural	33%	27%	40%	27%	33%
Urban	37%	29%	27%	12%	34%
Suburban	40%	34%	29%	17%	60%
UMC					
Rural	28%	50%	27%	25%	25%
Urban	58%	30%	41%	16%	56%
Suburban	68%	21%	31%	11%	37%
Presbyterian					
Rural	73%	36%	27%	9%	55%
Urban	66%	50%	16%	15%	54%
Suburban	50%	43%	7%	27%	57%

areas. Both urban and suburban areas reflect fewer new members than rural congregations.

When we consider Christian Methodist Episcopal church members, there is slight variation among the three locations in the numbers of college graduates, persons between eighteen and thirty-five, and persons over sixty years of age. A higher percentage of persons attending Christian Methodist Episcopal churches in urban areas is more likely to commute compared to rural and suburban areas.

There is no significant difference in the presence of African Methodist Episcopal Zion college graduates among the three locations. Rural churches have slightly higher percentages of persons between eighteen and thirty-five. A higher percentage of persons attending AMEZ congregations in suburban areas is more likely to commute over fifteen minutes to church than in rural and urban areas. New members are coming into the African Methodist Episcopal Zion church proportionally more often in the rural areas of the country.

There is a significant difference in the presence of Black United Methodist college graduates in suburban and urban areas as compared to the rural areas. Urban churches, as compared to suburban ones, have slightly higher percentages of persons between eighteen and thirty-five and over sixty years of age. Rural UMC congregations have large numbers of persons over sixty years of age. A higher percentage of persons attending UMC parishes in urban areas is more likely to commute over fifteen minutes to church than in rural and suburban areas. Rural congregations have a larger number of new members.

There is no significant difference in the length of commuting to church among rural, urban, and suburban churches in Presbyterian (U.S.A.) congregations. Rural churches have slightly higher percentages of persons between eighteen and thirty-five. Urban Presbyterian (U.S.A.) churches have the greatest numbers of people over sixty years of age. A higher percentage of Presbyterian (U.S.A.) churches in suburban areas have new members.

In the comparison of Black Baptist churches established before 1965 and since, the percentages vary significantly among the surveyed items (Fig. 2.4). However, little difference is noted in

Figure 2.4. Characteristics of Black Denominational Groups by Year Organized

	College Graduates	Age 60+	Ages 18–35	New Members	Commute 15+ Mins.
Baptist					
1965 and earlier	36%	26%	35%	18%	53%
1966–2000	25%	9%	44%	27%	55%
COGIC					
1965 and earlier	18%	15%	36%	18%	48%
1966–2000	20%	11%	37%	20%	48%
AME					
1965 and earlier	44%	33%	31%	17%	46%
1966–2000	29%	0%	29%	29%	74%
CME					
1965 and earlier	34%	30%	22%	13%	45%
1966–2000	22%	22%	48%	35%	73%
AMEZ					
1965 and earlier	35%	34%	28%	14%	50%
1966–2000	40%	10%	40%	30%	40%
UMC					
1965 and earlier	56%	30%	21%	11%	50%
1966–2000	60%	10%	40%	40%	40%
Presbyterian					
1965 and earlier	65%	46%	16%	14%	54%
1966–2000	45%	62%	25%	25%	50%

the length of commute. Among Church of God in Christ congregations there is very little difference in comparisons according to the time of church establishment. African Methodist Episcopal, Christian Methodist Episcopal, African Methodist Episcopal Zion, Black United Methodist Church and Black Presbyterian (U.S.A.) differ in all categories depending upon their time of establishment. Thus the Church of God in Christ denominational churches appear to have attracted characteristically similar members, whether they joined the church before 1966 or more recently. The other six denominational groups differ according to the time their churches were established.

National Census Comparisons

Overall this study of African American congregations has focused on just a few characteristics of their members, including percentages of college graduates, families with income below $20,000, eighteen- to thirty-five-year-olds, and persons over sixty years of age. The pastors or pastoral assistants of the approximately nineteen hundred churches in the survey identified their active members as being 14 percent college graduates, 9 percent living in families with an income below $20,000, 9 percent eighteen to thirty-five years of age, and 7 percent over sixty years of age (see Fig. 2.5).

But how do these characteristics compare to the total African American population? Are those men and women, boys and girls who attend Black churches with regularity proportionally similar to the general African American population? The answer is yes and no.

In terms of higher education, the data from Project 2000 is fairly similar to the general U.S. census, which counts approximately 16.5 percent of Black Americans who completed their college education in 1999. The seven denominational groups studied in this endeavor claimed approximately 14 percent.

As for men and women over sixty years of age, the figures for active church members and the national Black population in general are similar (7 percent and 11 percent respectively).

But when we examine family income below $20,000 and young people eighteen to thirty-five years of age, there are some significant differences. While the pastors reported that their churches counted approximately 9 percent of active members who live in families with incomes below $20,000, the U.S. census lists 21.9 percent of Black families as being below the poverty level. (A U.S. family of four whose total income is less than $18,400 in 2003

Figure 2.5. Comparison of Project 2000 Data
with U.S. Census Data for African Americans

	Project 2000	U.S Census*
EDUCATION		
College graduates	14%	16.5% (1999)
INCOME		
Family income below $20,000	9%	
Family income below poverty level		21.9% (1999)
AGE		
18–35	9%	
18–34		26% (2001)
Over 60	7%	
60 and over		11% (2001)

*U.S. Census Bureau, *Statistical Abstract of the United States, 2001,* 121st ed. (Washington, D.C., 2001).

is considered to be living below the poverty level.) These comparisons are not identical, but they do suggest that while certain families who are experiencing some level of economic restriction are in the local Black congregations, many must be somewhere else. Some may be attending a church other than the seven considered in this project, but others may not be active in any church, masjid, or synagogue.

Finally, it is evident that the African American community includes many young people; 26 percent are age eighteen to thirty-five according to the U.S. census 2001 projection. The Black Church has attracted some of these young adults (9 percent), but has not attracted many others. Reaching the younger generations is still a challenge in Black congregational life.

Lincoln and Mamiya devote an entire chapter to the topic of young people and the Black Church in their classic text on African American religiosity, *The Black Church in the African American Experience.* They suggest that the local church must address two major issues if Black children and youth are going to be helped in significant ways in the future: the ambivalence of racial identity and the problems of the Black underclass, especially as it impacts teenagers and young adults. African American young people need to discover or rediscover their strong racial heritage and identity. They need to claim their wholeness and history. The Black Church can help them do just that.[4] Jewelle Gibbs spoke of Black male youths as an "endangered species" when she looked at the condition and urban life.[5] "In many urban areas, as many as a third of Blacks between the ages of 17 and 21 are now under the jurisdiction of the criminal justice system."[6]

Black congregations can greatly assist in addressing these major community problems. It has in the past and can do so in the future. In fact, Andrew Billingsley, in his study of approximately one thousand Black churches, found that "the second most frequent type of program operated by Black churches after family-support programs is children and youth programs."[7] Black churches are designing programs to meet the needs of Black adolescents, but obviously more is needed.

Summary and Conclusion

Generally speaking, significant numbers of members of Black churches commute more than fifteen minutes to participate in their worship and other church-related activities. There is some membership growth occurring in all of the major Black denominations, less so with Black United Methodists and Black Presbyterians. Church of God in Christ congregations and Christian Methodist Episcopal churches tend to have larger percentages of families with incomes less than $20,000. Church of God in Christ churches, however, are attracting younger people more successfully than the other denominations. Black United Methodist churches have higher percentages of people over sixty years old, and Black Presbyterian (U.S.A.) have significantly more college graduates than the other denominations.

When we observe the seven Black denominations with regard to their setting, there are some significant differences to be noted (Fig. 2.3). Depending on their rural, urban, or suburban setting, different churches appear to draw different individuals — characteristically speaking. For example, college graduates in Black United Methodist churches are strikingly more in evidence in urban and suburban settings as compared to rural locations. New members are more often found in rural African Methodist Episcopal churches than their urban and suburban congregations. As we might expect, commuting is occurring more often in the urban and suburban areas for all churches.

When the seven denominational groups are considered according to the years their churches were organized, there does appear to be rather significant variance among them (Fig. 2.4). Among the seven denominational groups only one, the Church of God in Christ, does not show a significant change when the year of origin of the churches is considered.

Finally, percentages of college graduates and people sixty years of age and older in the various Black denominations are similar to national census trends. Percentages of people who are eighteen to thirty-five and those with family incomes below $20,000 are greater in the general population than in the Black churches.

3

THE BLACK CHURCH

IDENTITY, THEOLOGY, AND CULTURE

Identity in the Christian Community:
Who We Are and Whose We Are

The community that confesses Jesus as Lord has been from the beginning a movement launched into the public life of humankind. The Greco-Roman world was full of societies that offered those who wished to join a way of personal salvation through religious teaching and practice. The church by contrast was a movement claiming the allegiance of all people. The church was a different kind of *ecclésia,* the assembly of all citizens called together by the town clerk to deal with the public affairs of the city. The church was the assembly summoned not by the town clerk, but by God. It was *ecclésia Theou.* The scope of *ecclésia Théou* was much broader than any one city and its environs. It embraced the *oikoumené* — the whole inhabited earth, the world and all the peoples who dwell therein. The church has from the beginning understood its scope, life, work, and witness as in the public arena and for the public. The confirmation of this responsibility is the Resurrection of Jesus present and in the world where no Jewish council or Roman governor could stop His truth. The public nature of congregational life must always be upheld, proclaimed, and lived.

Congregational Life as Story:
Issues of Identity, Culture, and Theology

A generally accepted concept of the Christian congregation is that it is a gathered community of faith with a story — of individuals discovering and sharing life together and seeking to witness to the common story of their life together under God in Jesus Christ. The identity of each congregation is shaped by history, circumstance, and doctrine. Further distinctions are reflected in ethnicity, location, and culture. The ordered life in community is preparation for the life of mission in and to the world. When we do theology, we are not only, as individual Christians and communities of faith, talking about our life with God; we are seeking to walk with and according to the way of God.

The early Christians were known as followers of *hodos*, the way. Paul says the following of Jesus is a "walking according to the Spirit" who is life and who empowers us to make the journey. Every experience of following brings home to us the fact that there is no path marked out in advance in its every detail. There is no beaten path — one that has been traveled before. You know the way that you have to take as you pursue the journey.

Yet following Jesus, journeying with God, is not to go along a private route; it is rather a collective enterprise, with fellow Christians and in congregations. This is the biblical understanding of a people's journey in search of God. The Bible describes this "walking" as that of an entire people. It is a collective adventure under the prior action of the God who calls us out of the world, saves us, and sends us right back into the world to proclaim liberation to those who are bound. The journey is a community journey, and it is all-embracing; no dimension of human life is untouched. It expresses the concern and the saving action of God. Following Jesus entails a commitment to mission, which requires congregations, like the disciples, to pitch camp in the midst of human history and there give witness to God's love. It means that we have to respond to the world around us and the condition of people in that context. In congregational life, we are invited into structured conversations on God-talk, that is, theology. We are further challenged to make God-talk become God-walk and God-walk become God-talk.

In African American congregations there is much singing about God and much testifying about God in our lives. Stories are told of the God "who woke us up this morning, clothed in our right mind, and put food on our table, and shoes on our feet, who gave strength to our limbs." Sharing our common faith story becomes a way of strengthening individual and common life.

There is a connection between bringing men and women into a personal relationship with Jesus Christ and responsible church membership. The care of members within the fellowship of the congregation — how persons are accepted and find mutual support — is reflected in the way a congregation lives out its mission and ministry. The challenge and the call of congregational life is always a call to service in the world. Otherwise, we have only a club, a group of persons who share mutual interests, but not a fellowship of persons called together and empowered by the Holy Spirit. The internal nurture of community life is preparation for bold declaration of the lordship of Jesus and the evidence of that lordship in lives continually transformed so that all persons know the love and justice of God, whose Son died to redeem the world.

A New but Not Different Fellowship

Harold and Amanda Jackson and their two teenage children, Kenneth and Kenisha, were professionals moving back to the South after an extended residence in the Northeast. Originally from rural southern towns, they had gone to school in the North for undergraduate and graduate education. They met as undergraduates and married in their senior years. They were now well established in their professions. She was a nurse and an OR specialist. He was a lawyer, specializing in all aspects of business law.

They were now looking for a place to belong, to share their gifts, to experience a supportive atmosphere for their teenagers — a church home. They had heard about the great cathedral-like congregations that were emerging in the South, their spires piercing the sky like antennae seeking a connection with the divine.[8] The Jackson family found St. Philip. It was not a megachurch although it was a fairly large congregation in the metropolitan area. Under the leadership of the senior pastor, Dr. James, it had experienced significant growth over the previous decade so that the church had to relocate. The Jacksons' commute to church was no more than half an hour; the interstate highway system with which this metropolitan area was endowed assured easy access to church. They found St. Philip because the pastor was nationally known and because he had studied in seminary with their pastor in their congregation in the Northeast. Other families in that congregation had relatives who had made similar moves before them. Indeed, it appeared that St. Philip was becoming the new home for these transplants.

The diversity of programs offered not only contributed to the spiritual vitality of this congregation but was also attracting persons into its membership. Those who joined found a place for belonging and involvement. The Jacksons were particularly pleased that there was a strong youth ministry that enabled their teenagers to make a ready adjustment to their new environment and find new friends. The experience at St. Philip confirmed for Harold and Amanda that this was their spiritual home and that involvement in this congregation's life would be extremely meaningful as they continued their faith journey.

•

At the dawn of this new millennium our lives in society are increasingly characterized by bureaucratic control and depersonalizing technologies. Many persons are turning for deliverance to small groups where they experience deep interpersonal relationships with others who share their fundamental beliefs and values. Vital congregations provide many such possibilities for enhancing and enriching our common life.

There have been recurring statements about the spiritual vitality of congregations. Vital congregations have a clear sense of purpose and explicit member expectations that are strictly enforced. They have a positive assessment of the future. There is a distinct connection between clarity of purpose and the quality and quantity of financial support.[9]

There are a variety of sources of unity and cohesion that can help to solidify and strengthen congregational identity. The convergence of ethnic and religious identity can do this but can also be a mixed blessing. According to the FACT report approximately 60 percent of majority Latino congregations nationwide and half of majority Black congregations are "intentional about using their religious community as a resource for preserving their social/ethnic heritage. On the other hand, a distinct racial/ethnic identity can present a barrier to potential new members. Majority-white congregations with a distinct national identity ['white with subgroup' in Figure 3.1] are especially conscious about their need to increase their diversity."[10]

Denominational heritage or denominationalism can also assist in strengthening congregational identity. In the FACT study, among the forty-one denominational or faith groups surveyed, all

Figure 3.1. Preserving Racial/Ethnic/National Heritage: Percentage of Congregations High on Preservation

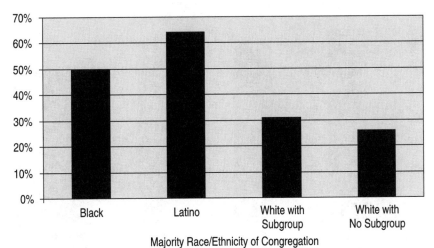

Majority Race/Ethnicity of Congregation

Source: Dudley and Roozen, *Faith Communities Today,* 16.

the groups held a deep commitment to denominational heritage (Fig. 3.2). In fact, all groups had a majority of its congregations recording a high level of commitment to the preservation of their heritage. The Black congregational bodies registered the highest level of support, almost 75 percent. This is obviously another factor that points to Black religious identity.

Clergypersons reported that their churches could be described as spiritually vital and alive (68 percent), as well as helping members deepen their relationship with God (66 percent) (Fig. 3.3). They perceived their members as being excited about the future (63 percent) and expressing a strong commitment to their denominational heritage (56 percent). On the whole, pastors or senior lay leaders of Black Presbyterian (U.S.A.) churches were far less likely than pastors or lay leaders of any of the other denominations studied to feel that any of the descriptions in figure 3.3 described their

Figure 3.2. Majority Racial/Ethnic/National Congregations Higher on Denominational Heritage

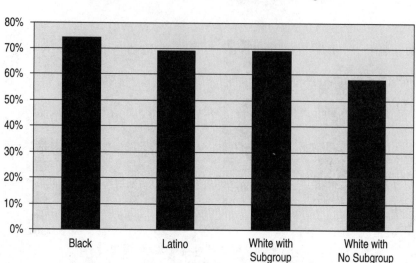

Majority Race/Ethnicity of Congregation

Source: Dudley and Roozen, *Faith Communities Today,* 17.

congregations "very well" (a "5" on a five-point scale). Indeed, only 38 percent of Black Presbyterian pastors and senior lay leaders felt that the statement "your congregation is spiritually vital and alive" described their congregation "very well" compared to 79 percent of Church of God in Christ pastors and 69 percent of the Baptists. This pattern emerged throughout the survey.

Assimilation or incorporation of new members into a local church is another important factor to consider in understanding the identity of a congregation. Generally speaking, African American congregations experienced some degree of growth during the period 1996–2000 (Fig. 3.4). Only a small percentage (8 percent) of Black churches report having lost membership, while approximately one-third (34 percent) have remained the same.

Figure 3.3. Pastoral Leaders' Description of Congregation by Percentage of Congregations

	Spiritually Vital and Alive	Working for Social Justice	Helps Members Deepen Relationship with God	Strong Commitment to Denominational Heritage	Excited about Future	Easily Assimilates New Members
Total	68%	43%	66%	56%	63%	39%
Baptist	69%	42%	67%	52%	66%	39%
COGIC	79%	46%	75%	61%	67%	45%
AME	62%	48%	61%	61%	56%	35%
CME	54%	37%	52%	55%	52%	36%
AMEZ	60%	46%	58%	61%	59%	37%
UMC	43%	33%	51%	44%	51%	21%
Presbyterian	38%	35%	45%	37%	40%	28%

Figure 3.4. Total Sample of Black Churches: Change in Size from 1996 to 2000

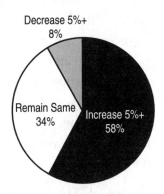

Nearly two-thirds of Baptist congregations (64 percent) and African Methodist Episcopal congregations (62 percent) indicated that they had experienced positive growth in the past five years (Fig. 3.5). The Presbyterians experienced less growth (40 percent

**Figure 3.5. Black Denominational Groups:
Change in Size from 1996 to 2000**

	Increase by 5%+	Remain the Same	Decrease by 5%+
Total Sample	58%	34%	8%
Baptist	64%	30%	6%
COGIC	56%	35%	9%
AME	62%	29%	9%
CME	52%	41%	7%
AMEZ	57%	33%	10%
UMC	60%	30%	10%
Presbyterian	40%	48%	12%

of the congregations) than the other Black denominational groups. In fact the Presbyterian pastors responding to this survey indicated that 12 percent of their churches had experienced a decrease in membership. The ease with which the clergy felt new persons were assimilated into their respective congregations differed somewhat among the seven Black denominational groups studied (Fig. 3.6). Overall new people were incorporated "very well" (38 percent) or "quite well" (32 percent). The Church of God in Christ leaders gave the most positive response (45 percent "very well") while the Presbyterian pastors (28 percent) and the United Methodists (21 percent) gave the least positive response. But generally the African American pastoral leadership surveyed in the study was positive regarding new member assimilation.

Finally, Black church leaders who viewed their congregations as spiritually vital were likely to characterize their congregations as:

- helping members deepen their relationship to God;
- being excited about the future of their congregation;
- assimilating new members into the life of the congregation;
- working for social justice; and
- strongly committed to its denominational heritage.

Figure 3.6. Incorporation of New Members into Black Denominational Groups, 1996–2000, by Percentage of Churches

	Very Well	Quite Well	Fairly Well	Not Well
Total Sample	39%	32%	23%	7%
Baptist	38%	34%	22%	5%
COGIC	45%	30%	22%	3%
AME	36%	32%	26%	6%
CME	36%	27%	24%	13%
AMEZ	38%	30%	24%	8%
UMC	21%	44%	21%	14%
Presbyterian	28%	33%	29%	10%

Culture and Assimilating New Members

The nature of our work and research permits us to be participant-observers at churches we visit. On one such visit, we noted that the worship was inviting and open. Persons felt free to participate: "When the pastor extends the invitation, if you want to, you may run down and holler." One member mentioned to us that visitors always comment on the feeling of love experienced during worship. He sensed no phoniness at the church and was made to feel welcome. "God used me to save my wife," he said, claiming that he led her into membership. "Now I am bringing other family members."

Congregations welcome new people all the time. When the preaching is done and the "doors of the church are opened," people respond. These persons will stay, however, as they are nurtured, assisted to learn the congregation's story, and made aware of its ethos. The level of teaching about heritage varies among the denominations. Most churches have some preparation and training process for new members. These include a history of the church, an explanation of its organization and structure, a presentation of the opportunities for ministry, instruction on the denominational heritage, and perspectives on stewardship, including the identifying, sharing, and managing of gifts, skills, and talents. Concerns for money are dealt with, and increasingly the concept of tithing is being presented in African American congregations. Many persons transfer from other denominations. Even those transferring from churches within the same denomination find these educational experiences refreshing, reaffirming, and inspirational. Where persons do not have these experiences and are not made to feel welcome, they cycle out of the life of that congregation as readily as they cycled in.

According to the FACT study, "Sociologists report that denominationalism is declining in significance for congregational identity.... One also finds that the expression of denominational heritage tends to be stronger in those congregations with a distinctive racial/ethnic/national identity."[11] There is much anecdotal evidence regarding the switching of denominations and an increasing loss of denominational loyalty. In one of our surveys in the dissemination phase of Project 2000, we learned that some churches have classes in denominational heritage especially for persons affiliating with that congregation from another denomination. This movement from one denomination to another, however, is more readily observable in the independent, nondenominational churches that are emerging across our nation. One study suggests that high levels of denominational switching are a characteristic of postwar generations whose loyalty to denomination is low.[12]

Summary and Conclusion

The identity of a person, as well as that of a congregation of people, is a critical concept. Churches have identities that help to shape their life together and their ministry in the community. They have a theological self-understanding and cultural heritage.

In many ways, every individual congregation or faith community has its own collective personality.

Speaking generally, African American congregations discover and rediscover who they are and whose they are as they work and worship together. They provide different resources for different people. Their ethnic and religious identity often fosters greater unity, and a cohesive denominational heritage greatly aids the process of identity formation and continuance. Many factors contribute to produce whole congregational life.

Spiritual vitality and great hope concerning the future is present in the contemporary Black Church. Pastors have reported that they feel good about the spiritual identity of their people. They believe that their congregants are deepening their relationship with God and are welcoming new people into the fold. They are upbeat about their current situation as it points to future ministry.

4

WORSHIP IN THE BLACK CHURCH

Sunday morning worship began at Mount Pleasant when brother James, the musician, went to the piano and struck chords that led the congregation in the popular song: "This Is The Day That the Lord Has Made." They slowly picked up the cues. Then Pastor Brockton added his call, as if stirring the tentativeness of the congregation to get started. The pastor had been at Mount Pleasant for nearly a decade. They knew him and he knew them. So when he suggested that they could do better than that, they understood where he was coming from. He continued, "Every day is the Lord's day. Let's give God some praise for this day that God had given us." The congregation responded; they got the message. Perhaps the Spirit began to descend at Mount Pleasant and move among the saints. The music got louder and the sanctuary began to vibrate. The session went on for twenty minutes. Spiritual vitality is exciting and inspiring when the whole congregation participates and the preacher's ability to tell the story evokes "Amens" and much applause.

A Window into the Black Worship Experience

At Mount Pleasant it was decidedly a Black Church worship experience that ran the range of denominational expressions. There

42

was the deacons' pre-worship of the Baptists; the "praise time" of the COGICs was informal but evident. A liturgical dance by the Deliverance Dancers was listed on the worship bulletin; they did not show and there was no explanation. Emphasis was placed on a "Time for Giving." The idea of "Not equal giving, but equal sacrifice" was bannered in a corner of the sanctuary.

The visiting preacher was a judicatory staff person. She worked her text very well and evoked affirmations of assent and agreement from the congregation. The sermon was a narrative exposition of Luke 7:36–50, the story of Jesus and "a woman in the city, who was a sinner." The preacher claimed that Jesus "reclining" at Simon's house illustrated his humanity. She invited us to note what preceded this reclining was an intense period of activity in which he helped persons. While *men* were socializing in the Pharisee's house this *woman* presses her way in. "I wonder how Simon knows that this woman is a sinner," asks the preacher. For nearly forty minutes she retold the story with commentary and inferences that challenged the hearers to self-examination.

The Liturgy and Its Flow:
Form and Function

Much of the vitality in African American congregational life is a result of an observable rhythmic flow that may be described in three incremental or gradual movements: approach to God, the Word of God, and response to God.

The *approach* may take a variety of forms. One of its manifestations is a session of praise time, most common in the Church of God in Christ, but not exclusive to this group. Praise time is not new; indeed it is part of Black worship that is being revived. Then there may be a deacon-led preparatory session preceding the appointed hour for worship. More general is the pattern that includes hymn, call to worship, and invocation.

The Word of God is offered through the reading or proclamation of the Scripture and the sermon, which is sometimes considered the central expression of the Word. Valentino Lassiter expresses strong and persistently held sentiments when he writes,

> Preaching in the African American tradition remains a most important element of the worship experience.... The people of God, there so gathered, sit in anticipation to learn just what the Word is saying for the day. The songs of Zion also did indeed speak to the soul. The loving fellowship of kindred spirits is very significant. Yet, the momentous spiritual event occurs in that special place and time as the person of God expounds upon life-sustaining truths and spiritual suggestions with a keen sense of theological soundness.[13]

The third observable movement in the liturgy may be described as *response to God*. This is expressed through a hymn of invitation or dedication, when persons are invited to respond as "the doors of the church are open." Intercessory prayer follows. This may take the form of persons being invited to the communion rail to make their petitions known to God. The order is interchangeable for the other elements in the service—the offering of gifts, tithes, special collections, and notices.

What Is the Word from the Lord?

We explored the focus of sermons with one pastor on a visit to his congregation. He expressed a belief that sermons need to address the spiritual issues of the times with guidance from the Word of God. The challenge is to relate the spiritual issues to those with which men and women are struggling every day. And because the

Church is in the world, the major sociopolitical issues also demand our attention. "If the Gospel is not social, it is irrelevant, for we are social creatures."

•

Trouble had arisen in the church at Corinth. The controversy was about the relation between moral discipline and Christian belief. There were other points up for discussion. But then persons started questioning the kind of authority that the apostle Paul had over the life and decisions of the Corinthian church that he had helped to found. The result of all of this was much confusion and misunderstanding and the emergence of factions in the church.

St. Paul cuts through all of that and gives a straight answer. "We speak the plain truth," he says, "and so commend ourselves to every man's conscience in the sight of God. If our gospel is 'veiled,' the veil must be in the mind of those who are spiritually dying. The spirit of this world has blinded the minds of those who do not believe, and prevents the light of the glorious gospel of Christ, the image of God, from shining on them. For it is Christ Jesus the Lord whom we preach, not ourselves; we are your servants for His sake" (2 Cor. 4:2–5, Phillips paraphrase). The preacher is not essentially a performer, but a witness. The calling is to be servant.

St. Paul does not hesitate to deny that any blame should be attached to him. "If our Gospel is 'veiled,'" he asserts, "the veil must be in the mind of those who are spiritually dying." It is not that the apostle is unaware of his own flawed and imperfect humanity. He writes very plainly, "It is not that I am personally qualified to form any judgment by myself; my qualifications come from God, and he has further qualified me to be the minister of a new covenant.... This treasure [is] in a frail vessel of earth" (2 Cor. 3:5–6; 4:7a.) In other words, the problem in the church at Corinth was not fundamentally a problem caused by a clash of opinions or personalities. It was rather a problem caused by unbelief. Out of all this, Paul could speak with confidence because he could lay claim to two incontestable facts. First of all, his preaching had been about Jesus Christ and no one else. "It is Jesus Christ as Lord that I proclaim," he says.

> Your contentions are not about *me* or with me, but about Him — Jesus Christ and with Him. He is both your Lord and mine. I did not seek in His name to lord it over you. You ought to deal directly with Him. Indeed, you must. In the second instance, "I am simply a servant of yours for Jesus' sake." He, who is *my* Lord and whose servant I am, made me *your* servant. I became a servant "through Him" (R.V. margin). He put me under submission to Him, and therefore, just as your controversy is not with me, neither can my controversy be with you. In all my dealings with you, whatever you say about me or do to me, I am still your servant. Jesus made me that, and that I must continue to be. But what is exciting and comforting for me is that "as I hold this ministry by God's mercy to me, I never lose heart in it." (See Moffatt's translation)

The pastor or minister is not a servant to do what the local church wants done simply because they demand it. Pastoral leaders do what they are convinced is demanded of them because Jesus Christ is the one who called them into ministry and they are servants to those among whom their journey is set. Whether the service offered is accepted or not, pastors cannot quit. They have been appointed "servants," and life among the people of God in any congregation is always service "for Jesus' sake."

There are many illustrations in the Gospel of the nature of this service. In John's Gospel, Jesus deals with the dispute among his disciples about place and position. He gets up from supper, girds himself with a towel, and washes his disciples' feet. Commenting on this incident the evangelist says, "Jesus, knowing that the Father had given all things into his hands, and that he had come from God and was going to God, rose from supper, laid aside his garments, and girded himself with a towel" (John 13:3–4). The garments of the Master are laid aside. He takes the form of a servant. As servant, he came from God, and as servant he must return to God. There is for him no remission from the servant's tasks.

Preachers and pastors are called to be servants, called to share in and continue the servant ministry of Jesus Christ. To speak of the Church as the extension of the ministry of Jesus Christ is to describe the Church's true identity. The Body of Christ is Christ present in his ongoing work. We are members of that body, congregants as well as pastors. "Servants of Jesus Christ," "servants through Jesus Christ," "servants for Christ's sake": those then are the preacher's credentials. That is what preachers are: servants to the Lord to whom they owe obedience and servants to the people God has entrusted into their hands for care and to whom service must be rendered. "For you were called to freedom, brothers and sisters," writes St. Paul. "Only do not use your freedom as opportunity for self-indulgence, but through love become slaves to one another" (Gal. 5:13). Barclay's translation is extremely pointed: " 'You must love your neighbor as yourself.' But if you snap at one another and devour one another, you must watch that you do not end up by wiping each other out" (Gal. 5:14–15).

Praising God in Zion

In the African American experience each historical era has helped the people to tell their story. In Africa and in the African Diaspora, songs emerged in the context of celebrations and festivals, songs that always included praise to the Supreme Being or God. In the slave period, the "sorrow" songs were forged out of the crucible of pain and suffering. For the slave ancestors those songs were affirmations of God, who sustained the people in spite of the brutality and dehumanization that they experienced. Through those spirituals slaves sang of a hope that "trouble don't last always." It is biblical hope that the Psalmist expressed after raising questions about God that evoked praise (Ps. 42:11; 43:3–4).

Music, which enhances the worship and is an important part of the flow of the liturgy, is more than organ and piano these days. There are also small orchestral ensembles, sometimes heavily weighted on the percussion side. Melva Wilson Costen observes that

> even with increases in diversified ministries and congregational involvement in the total life of the community, spawned by faith experiences in worship, fresh ways of praising God in Jesus the Christ will burst forth in new and old ways of singing, preaching, praying, and offering thanks. The liturgy, God's work through the people, will continue through drama, dance, and the sharing of songs across cultures.[14]

William McClain has contended,

> Worship in the black tradition is complex and contradictory realities. The sacred and the secular, Saturday night and Sunday morning, come together to affirm God's wholeness, the unity of life and his lordship over all of life. Such a tradition encourages responses of spontaneity and improvisation, and urges worshipers to turn themselves loose into the hands of the existential here and now where joy and travail mingle together as part of the reality of God's creation. It is in this context that black people experience the life of faith and participate in the community of faith.[15]

Sermon Topics, Music, and Other Worship Activities

When the ministers were asked about the topics of their sermons, the overwhelming majority felt that their sermons "always" focus on God's love and care (83 percent), personal spiritual growth (74 percent) and practical advice on daily living (66 percent) (Figure 4.1) Comparatively few indicated that their sermons almost always focus on social justice (25 percent), the social situation (17 percent) or Black liberation theology or womanist theology (12 percent). Black United Methodist (57 percent) and Black Presbyterian (46 percent) ministers were less likely than others interviewed to report that their sermons "always" focus on practical advice for daily living and spiritual growth. No statistically significant differences emerged among congregations of different sizes in regard to sermon focus; small, medium, and large churches reported approximately the same emphases in their sermons.

Figure 4.1. Sermon Topics "Always" Focused Upon by Percentage of Black Pastors

	God's Love and Care	Practical Advice for Daily Living	Personal Spiritual Growth	Social Justice and Social Activism	Racial Situations in Society	Liberation Theology or Womanist Theology
Total	83%	66%	74%	25%	17%	12%
Baptist	84%	66%	74%	24%	17%	10%
COGIC	85%	68%	76%	27%	17%	11%
AME	80%	61%	75%	26%	18%	14%
CME	85%	66%	73%	32%	23%	19%
AMEZ	87%	72%	74%	26%	22%	18%
UMC	80%	57%	64%	23%	14%	13%
Presbyterian	70%	46%	55%	14%	9%	7%

Figure 4.2. Elements Always Included in Black Worship by Percentage of Congregations

	Spirituals	Modern Gospel	Gospel Rap	Dance or Drama
Total	52%	29%	1%	9%
Baptist	53%	30%	1%	8%
COGIC	62%	31%	1%	15%
AME	41%	29%	2%	6%
CME	55%	26%	2%	6%
AMEZ	47%	29%	1%	6%
UMC	30%	19%	1%	4%
Presbyterian	21%	12%	1%	1%

About half of all clergy members (52 percent) reported that spirituals are "always" included in their services (Figure 4.2). There were wide differences, as expected, among denominational groups. While over half of Baptist, Church of God in Christ, and Christian Methodist Episcopal clergy reported that they always included spirituals in their services, only 21 percent of Black Presbyterians and 30 percent of Black United Methodists reported that to be the case. Some differences emerged on the basis of educational background. Churches that had pastors with a seminary degree or higher education were less likely to use spirituals in their services than those with no formal training or some Bible college or some ministry training.

Modern gospel music was always included in services for relatively few clergypersons (29 percent). Dance or drama, while not part of all services, was included in at least some services while very few included gospel rap as part of their services.

The study included a section on worship elements (Figure 4.3). Sacred scripture (characterized as "extremely important" by 60 percent of the respondents) and the presence of the Holy Spirit (67 percent) were the elements considered to be the most

Figure 4.3. Elements Characterized as "Extremely Important" in Worship and Teaching, by Percentage of Congregations

	Sacred Scripture	Historical Creeds, Doctrines, Traditions	Presence of the Holy Spirit	Personal Experience
Total	60%	26%	67%	39%
Baptist	61%	21%	67%	40%
COGIC	61%	30%	71%	42%
AME	60%	30%	64%	35%
CME	56%	33%	61%	39%
AMEZ	66%	36%	69%	46%
UMC	50%	18%	56%	37%
Presbyterian	61%	19%	50%	28%

important aspects in the worship and teaching of the congregations. Historical creeds, doctrines, and traditions, as well as personal experience, while considered important, were not at the top of the list.

In the FACT study "uplifting worship and spiritual nurture" made "a genuine contribution to congregational growth in every congregational group" studied.[16] Contemporary forms of worship, associated with electronic musical instruments, rather than traditional forms seemed to be most effective in supporting church growth. Churches and faith communities that have changed their worship patterns or styles most often in recent years tended to be the older churches located in metropolitan areas. In many cases, the large, predominately Black congregations of the U.S. cities are making significant changes in their worship to attract new individuals and families. "The impact of change in contemporary worship is clear.... Changes in worship patterns, especially in using new instruments (electric guitar and electronic keyboard, for example) have a strong, positive association with congregational vitality, member growth, financial stability and other signs of a healthy congregation."[17] This pattern was affirmed in the examination of all the faith communities in the FACT national survey. It rings true with regard to our experience of Black congregations, especially those in urban areas with significant numbers of members.

Lincoln and Mamiya speak of a "neo-Pentecostal" form of worship that has attracted Black urban poor congregations in recent years. "Neo-Pentecostalism in Black churches tends to draw upon the reservoir of the Black folk religious tradition which stressed enthusiastic worship and Spirit-filled experiences. One of the appeals of the current movement is its emphasis on a deeper spirituality and the need for a second blessing of the Holy Spirit.[18] They are alerting the Black Church, especially its more mainline Protestant denominations, to pay attention to these new or restructured forms of worship. Whether we are considering changes in musical instruments and worship, or Spirit-filled activities in Sunday morning gatherings of Black people, the future provides some new possibilities for the twenty-first-century African American church.

Summary and Conclusions

Worship is at the center of Black congregational life. The people gathered for spiritual sustenance are empowered to share their gifts and graces with those beyond their worship settings. The word preached and responded to is of utmost importance. Music and musical movement in the worship encounter is essential. The Scripture read, historical creeds affirmed, and practical advice given in the Spirit-led assembly of African American men, women, and children confirms the place and relevance of the Black Church in today's world.

5

INSIDE BLACK CONGREGATIONAL LIFE

In the African American experience, Bible study has for a long time been associated with Wednesday nights — a midweek event that churches were expected to have if there were no other events until the following Sunday. It was different when Pastor Yancey came to First Baptist. He instituted a Saturday morning Bible study that lasted for two hours. Like most changes, this one met resistance. People found all kinds of excuses to be absent. But word began to thread its way through the congregation that some exciting things were happening. People were being asked to study the selected passages during the week and were permitted to share their insights and discoveries, what they felt the Word meant to them in their lives in their families, in their church, and alongside their fellow human beings in the world. It was different all right. The previous pastors had spent most of their time telling the folk what the Word was saying. Pastor Yancey was acknowledging that God through the Holy Spirit could and did lead persons into the truth — and not only the pastor. God is God's own interpreter and God makes the Word plain.

•

Vincent Wimbush has made a significant contribution to our understanding of the Bible. He has proposed that we think of the

Bible as language, even a language-world. The slaves acquired this language as a skill for survival. The Bible became a means through which they negotiated both the strange new world that was called America and the slave existence. With this "language" they began to wax eloquent about the ways in which they understood their situation in America — as slaves, as freed persons, as disenfranchised persons, as a people. For the great majority of African Americans the Bible has functioned historically not merely to reflect and legitimize piety (narrowly understood), but as a language-world full of stories — of heroes and heroines, of heroic peoples and their pathos and victory, sorrow and joy, sojourn and fulfillment. In short, the Bible became a "world" into which African Americans could retreat, a "world they could identify with, draw strength from, and in fact manipulate for their self-affirmation."[19]

Participation in Religious Programs

There is a long history of internal nurture for survival in the Black faith community, but it has never been to the exclusion of reaching out. Indeed, the inward nurture was preparation for going out to live one's faith in community, seeking to promote and establish love and justice in God's world.

Congregations pursue their lives in a variety of ways and generally through activities that fall into the areas of worshiping, caring, learning, and serving. Different groups, programs, and ministries enable them to invite and receive people as they are and assimilate persons into their community of faith. Evangelistic efforts seek to reach out to bring new persons into fellowship and membership. Persons find relationship with God in prayer meetings, spiritual retreats, and small faith-sharing groups, to name a few. The Holy Spirit initiates and sustains this relationship. Educational experiences, including Bible study, membership preparation classes, doctrinal study groups, and forums on social issues, help persons not only to learn about their denominational heritage but also to grow in faithfulness and obedience as disciples for their Christian journey. When there are persons who are sick or in crisis, individuals and groups provide loving care for one another.

Through many service-oriented programs, members are prepared and equipped to live out their faith, responding to a world that needs to know and experience God's justice. Congregation are called to act from the center of their own life, the culture that has been shaped through their history and the beliefs and values that their members embrace. The ongoing challenge is to identify the needs, evaluate the capacity for response, and act always with the awareness that God who has called us into being as people of God will equip us for the life to which we have been called.

Building Community for Common Work

Community enables persons to find themselves, their gifts, and their place in the economy of common life. Community is central to the African American heritage.

> In the cotton fields and plantations of the South, African Americans labored from sunup to sundown, singing as they worked. Participating in singing and music making was not only a form of community experience; it also served to provide power for arduous labor. Indeed, music making helped to invite African Americans into a participatory group activity for a common purpose. And on the plantation, it helped to get the work done.[20]

Congregations need to take time to identify persons in their fellowship who have gifts, skills, and commitment to offer in a common mission.

Figure 5.1. Black Church Participation in Religious Programming
over a One-Year Period, by Percentage of Congregations
Reporting Programs

	Bible Studies Other Than Sunday School	Theological or Doctrinal Studies	Prayer or Meditation Groups	Spiritual Retreats
Total	98%	75%	93%	64%
Baptist	99%	77%	95%	67%
COGIC	97%	78%	95%	60%
AME	98%	69%	90%	65%
CME	95%	67%	90%	64%
AMEZ	99%	76%	93%	70%
UMC	97%	60%	86%	61%
Presbyterian	97%	62%	88%	59%

One of the New Testament descriptions of the Christian community is "household of God" (Eph. 2:19), a notion consonant with African perspectives on belonging, affirmation, and relationship. An Akan proverb illustrates this concept of community: "If a thorn gets into the toe, the whole body bends to pluck it out."

The Greek word *okeioi* is derived from *oikos,* house. The adjective *oikeios* means one's own rather than another's — domestic, family, intimate, kin. It also means fit for, appropriate to, belonging to, the very nature or essence of a thing. The Old Testament word *bayith* in reference to God usually refers to the covenant people of God and the *place* where they gather for worship.

In the United States we speak of sorority or fraternity houses. The president lives in the White House. Our federal government does its business in the Congress, one part of which is the House of Representatives. In the plantation economy of our earlier history, and particularly during the slave period, there were the great houses. Slaves who worked in the master's house were referred to as house slaves as distinguished from field slaves, those who labored in the fields.

Figure 5.1 (continued). Black Church Participation in Religious Programming over a One-Year Period, by Percentage of Congregations Reporting Programs

	Community Services	Parenting or Marriage Enrichment	Youth Programs	Young adult or Singles Programs
Total	91%	67%	96%	72%
Baptist	92%	67%	96%	74%
COGIC	88%	75%	95%	73%
AME	94%	65%	97%	70%
CME	88%	51%	92%	71%
AMEZ	96%	64%	97%	71%
UMC	94%	60%	94%	61%
Presbyterian	94%	35%	91%	46%

All these usages of "house" imply communities, structures, and institutions. The word "economics" derives from the Greek word that means management of the household; economics is a kind of national housekeeping. A fundamental task of every congregation is to enable persons, not only to discover themselves and their gifts, skills, and talents, but to find ways to share, and manage those gifts and skills to further the mission and ministry of that congregation.

Religious and Social Programs

Most clergypersons interviewed reported that their congregations participated in a wide range of religious and social programs during the previous year (1999–2000) (Figure 5.1). More than nine in ten congregations participated in Bible study, prayer or meditation groups, community services, and youth programs. Large majorities participated in the other activities examined: spiritual retreats, parenting and marriage enrichment, theological study, and young adult and singles programs. Chapter 6 will highlight the details of community outreach and social programs.

Small Groups
and Congregational Life

There is plenty of opportunity in small groups for discovering one another's stories and entering into the life of others in ways that can strengthen individual and common life. But we have discovered that the best functioning small groups are those in which the members care deeply about one another. They interact with one another during the week. If one of them is in distress — a teenage driver wrecks a car — all the members know about it. If one is in the hospital, they all go to see her. The group is a primary life-support system.

There are also open groups where people are not looking in at each other but are all looking out. There are such groups in every church. They are often formed by appointment. Somebody, usually the pastor or a nominations and personnel committee, selects persons and puts them together for a task, for example, the Committee on Interfaith Relations. It is often difficult for the group to get started. Someone asks, "Who is going to be the chairperson?" Silence. "We need a secretary. Who will be our secretary? I think you should do the job, Mavis." When you have groups like this in your church, you may never get things done. If the task gets done, however, it is because the members go through the ritual of *forming,* and then the process of *storming* (discovering one another and what each can contribute to the task) and *norming* (covenanting to commit to the task), and finally *performing.* Once the norming has taken place, the group becomes closed and it becomes difficult to embrace others. Members subsequently develop the characteristics of a closed group as they learn of the lives of others and set about their common task.

A congregation that is alive should have several groups that are closed and many new groups that are continually forming. Every new member should be given an opportunity to become actively involved in some small group within the life of the church. Where this is happening, the congregation is on the way to becoming a vital and committed community where the faithful are affirmed, have a sense of belonging, and grow in meaningful relationships in their faith journey.

Programs and Leadership

Clergy who were paid pastors, either full- or part-time, rather than serving as volunteers, were more likely to be involved in the activities and programs examined. Moreover, the larger the congregation, the more likely they were to be involved in virtually all of the activities or programs listed.

In the FACT study, when all denominational and faith groups were considered, certain denominations gave evidence of distinctive patterns that reflect their social and religious heritage. For example:

- Catholic/Orthodox congregations more frequently sponsor programs of theological or doctrinal training, spiritual retreats, and programs for young adults, and marriage enrichment;

- historically Black churches are more likely to emphasize prayer groups and opportunities for community service;

- liberal and moderate Protestants more distinctively support opportunities for community services and the arts; and

- Evangelical Protestants are strong in support of prayer groups.[21]

Regular Program Evaluation and Reenvisioning the Future

Congregations follow some design and they discover their identity, understand their history, chart their position on a life cycle, define their mission, carry out that mission, and engage in ministry. As programs are developed and move purposively to fulfill their goals, they should engage in regular and ongoing evaluation. A basis for such evaluation is found in goals set and outcomes anticipated. Additionally, check-ups need to be made of human and material resources that are available, the level of commitment and enthusiasm of those involved, and strategies to effect action proposed. Failures along the way need to be noted, and opportunities for celebration of achievement need to be planned. As leaders and congregations design and follow through on plans for evaluating their work, they will learn that faithfulness and obedience enable ministry that brings glory to God.

Summary and Conclusion

Individual and family participation in the congregational life of Black churches takes many forms, enabling members to be nurtured and cared for as they nurture and care for those within and beyond their church doors. Bible study, beyond Sunday school classes, is taken seriously by almost all African American parishioners. Theological and doctrinal studies, prayer and meditation are equally important. Black churches maintain programs and sponsor events that support youth and young adults. Community service is a great priority.

Human beings long for connectedness. Black congregational life provides a rhythm of connectedness for the journey inward and the journey outward.

6

COMMUNITY OUTREACH THROUGH THE BLACK CHURCH

Black churches have a long history of serving their communities — both their members and those beyond their doors who are not on the membership roll.

Outreach is a natural, essential characteristic of African American congregations. African American congregations very readily identify with people in their context, especially the neediest and most neglected. The Black Church understands that the choice for Jesus Christ is equally a decision for people. There is no way to talk and sing and shout about "loving Jesus" and not love one's neighbor, the one for whom Jesus died. There is an overriding conviction that people matter.

This commitment to people in all their sundry situations of need expresses what was described a generation ago as an "option for the poor." This concern for taking care of persons is expressed through a variety of means. Our research documents the imaginative and concrete responses to human need, and the FACT report affirmed that "when it comes to the willingness of congregations to go beyond service and become involved in organized social issue advocacy or community organizing, historically Black churches rate both issues more highly than other faith groups."[22]

The Church is essentially ex-centric. It is God's purpose that the Church move out from the center of its own life to the margins of compassionate concern, where the Lord is already at work. The challenge is ongoing for Black churches, as well as all religious bodies committed to helping people in disadvantaged and distressing situations. There is need to find ways to maximize participation of individuals and groups in congregations. This commitment becomes meaningful as congregations come to grips with the community among whom their journey is set. They must become critically aware of their community so that their witness is determined by the hard knowledge of concrete realities of the human condition. Congregations must identify with and serve the poor, heal the blind and the sick, and engage in the process of liberating the oppressed.

Numerous scholars, denominational leaders, and local pastors have documented the rich and varied history of community outreach and service of the Black churches. Lincoln and Mamiya describe in depth the multiple and varied forms of African American generosity and Black Church community outreach. "Mutual aid or beneficial societies and churches were among the first social institutions created by Black people. They often existed in a symbiotic relationship. Sometimes mutual aid societies led to the formation of Black churches, and at other times societies were organized under the rubric of the churches."[23] Whatever the case, the Black Church has in many ways modeled an important social reality in the United States. It has taken seriously the needs of its people, communities, and nation. It has reached out to others in significant and meaningful ways.

In *No Hiding Place: Empowerment and Recovery for Our Troubled Communities,* Cecil Williams and Rebecca Laird illustrate how one large Black United Methodist Church in the Tenderloin area of San Francisco reached out to Black men and women who were seemingly crippled by substance abuse problems.[24] Under Reverend Williams's leadership that church has made an incredible impact on that city and beyond. The church has demonstrated how masses of people can be empowered for their own and society's welfare.

In her book *Servants of the People: The 1960s Legacy of African American Leadership*, Lea E. Williams gives six historical examples of servant leadership involving community outreach and development.[25] A. Phillip Randolph, Frederick D. Patterson, Thurgood Marshall, Whitney M. Young Jr., Adam Clayton Powell Jr., and Fannie Lou Hamer, highlighted by Williams, mirror the power and presence of Black church and community service.

In a similar fashion, Ronald Nored describes how African American and other congregations can work together to build their neighborhoods. A current example of Black Church coalition building and neighborhood development is flourishing in Birmingham:

In the fall of 1990, the six-block neighborhood in the Ensley section of Birmingham, Alabama, known as Sandy Bottom was filled with decaying, substandard, shotgun style houses. The utility lines leading to the houses drooped down to within five feet of the ground in many yards. Everywhere there were trash-filled, vacant lots scattered throughout the neighborhood. The streets were narrow and often muddy from lack of adequate drainage sewers. Drug traffic, economic decline, absentee landlords, and inadequate social services troubled residents daily. Sandy Bottom's residents had all but given up hope for this historic, but now dying, neighborhood.

In the fall of 1996, the same six-block neighborhood, renamed Sandy Vista, saw the completion of the thirtieth new home on its recently widened streets, streets that now boasted new curbs and drainage sewers. Newly installed sidewalks are well lit by modern street lights, and the last of the shot-gun homes has been demolished to make way for the next house in the sixty-four home development. Residents are now homeowners and members of the Sandy Vista Residents As-sociation, the organization primarily responsible for making all decisions about the future of the neighborhood.[26]

Other documentation could be presented here, but these few examples illustrate a central contention of this book, namely, that the Black Church and its people have been and continue to be active participants in community outreach and development.

Context and Mission

Every congregation is located in a particular geographic commu-nity for which it must accept responsibility as an arena for mission and ministry. It lives its life at a particular period in time, and con-text and time are significant factors that affect a congregation's life. Where these influences are not acknowledged and affirmed, a con-gregation lives for itself, behind closed doors, unconcerned about the realities of its life and the world around it. Congregations have the capacity to affect their context through the ways in which they organize themselves and engage their context. Conversely the en-vironment in which they find themselves affects and shapes the lives of congregations. Contextually aware congregations:

- have a healthy self-awareness and understanding of themselves;

- seek to hold institutions in their contexts accountable for the welfare of all persons, particularly the poor and helpless and hopeless;

- are committed to working with other churches, agencies, and interest groups that struggle for justice;

- live the life of faith beyond the walls and in the world;

- engage in analysis through reflection and action.

As James A. Forbes Jr. remarks, "Conversations about social transformation really begin to be significant when the people discussing the issue speak specifically about the vision that inspires their hope; when they articulate the programmatic thrust they propose; and when they describe the source of power and sustenance available to those who commit themselves to the implementation of world-changing plans."[27] Persons seek opportunities to talk about their deepest concerns. When they get together and engage in discussion, they discover and share their feelings, beliefs, and values. They also begin to explore ways in which they can respond and begin to effect changes in conditions about which they are dissatisfied.

Through our ministry as Christians with persons in our world, we witness to Jesus as Savior and Lord with our words and our deeds. We who bear his name come under the searching light of God's judgment on all persons, and that judgment begins with us. We are called to raise some self-evaluative questions about our mission and ministry as congregations and communities of faith: Do we love persons enough to be able to witness to them or instead will our witness be false testimony? Can God confirm our witness? Do we believe and live our belief that Jesus Christ died for all persons and not only for us who profess faith in him.

Recent Research in Community Outreach

One of the superior accounts of African American social outreach in and beyond the Black Church is Andrew Billingsley's *Mighty*

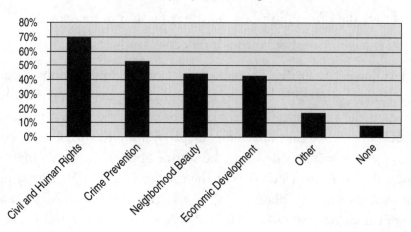

Figure 6.1. Areas of Black Church Involvement
in the Community, by Percentage of Churches

Source: *A Study on Financing African American Churches: National Survey on Church Giving* (Atlanta: Institute of Church Administration and Management, 1997)

Like a River: The Black Church and Social Reform.[28] Billingsley uniquely describes the evolution of the Black Church as an agent of social reform and gives numerous present-day examples of the way the Black Church continues to reach out to the community. Billingsley's research and writing is based, in part, on a comprehensive study of approximately one thousand Black churches in the United States. He details how community outreach is of critical importance to the Black religious experience. And while there is significant variation of outreach, that priority is present in Black congregational life.

In a more recent study directed by the Institute of Church Administration and Management (ICAM) on giving patterns among African American churches, it was confirmed that Black churches across the United States were significantly involved in their respective communities.[29] Seventy-four of the 141 churches examined in the ICAM study were involved in some type of community service project. Food and feeding programs (70 percent), clothes closets (31 percent), youth camping/scouting (20 percent), tutoring/ mentoring (15 percent), and drug abuse counseling (15 percent) were some of the areas of service mentioned by the respondents in that study.

In addition to the service programs they provided, nearly all (92 percent) of the 141 churches were involved in some kind of community action around issues affecting the entire community. These community concerns included advocating for civil rights, neighborhood crime prevention, neighborhood beautification, and economic development projects to generate local commerce and employment (Figure 6.1). Only 8 percent of the churches examined in the ICAM national survey on church giving were not involved in some kind of community action. Almost three-quarters (72 percent) of the churches provided free space on church grounds for community activities. These 141 Black churches for the most part gave convincing evidence of their intentions to be available to and supportive of the various communities within which they were located. We found this to be even more the case in our examination of more than eighteen hundred Black churches nationwide.

Most of the African American clergypersons interviewed in our study reported that their congregations participated in a wide range of religious and social programs during the previous year (2000) (Figure 6.2). At least three-fourths of all Black churches surveyed sponsored youth programs (92 percent); cash assistance to families or individuals (86 percent); voter registration or voter education (76 percent); and food pantries or soup kitchens (75 percent). When we take into account that congregations in the historically Black denominations tend to have more members from low-income households, the cash assistance and food pantry/soup kitchen programs suggest that African American churches set as a

Figure 6.2. Black Church Sponsorship of Social Services/
Community Programs, 2000, by Percentage of
Congregations Involved

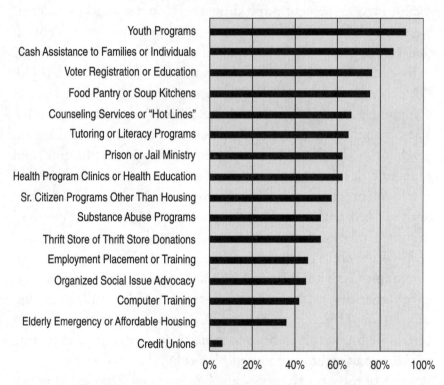

priority their members and their communities. They are spiritual communities serving the common good.

Interestingly, when compared to all other faith groups, whether liberal Protestant, moderate Protestant, evangelical Protestant, Catholic, Orthodox, and other world religious bodies (Baha'is, Mormons, and Muslims), the historically Black Protestant churches provide more outreach programs than any of the other groups (Figure 6.3). In many ways, community service is as much an expression of faith in the Black Church as Bible study and prayer groups.

Figure 6.3. Faith Groups and Range of Outreach Ministries, by Average Number of Outreach Programs

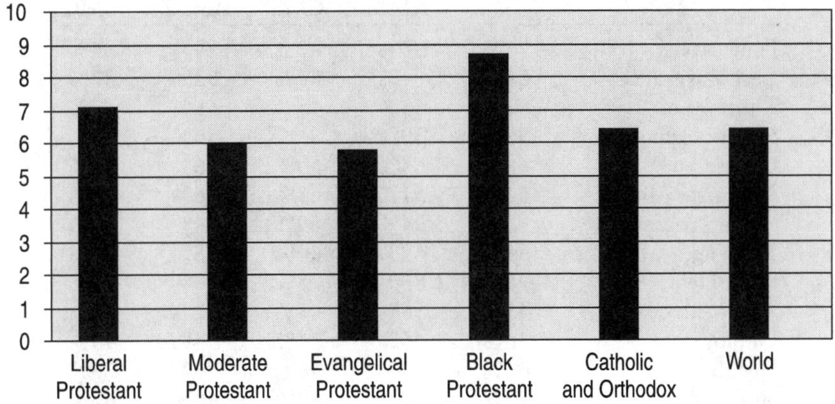

Source: Dudley and Roozen, *Faith Communities Today*, 48.

Although approximately 45 percent of all Black churches are involved in social advocacy overall, African Methodist Episcopal Zion churches (62 percent) and Black United Methodist congregations (63 percent) are far more likely to report this involvement (Figure 6.4). This same denominational pattern emerges regarding sponsorship of health programs and clinics.

As we might expect, larger congregations sponsor a greater variety of social service programs for the needy in the community. Larger churches tend to have more staff and greater financial resources than smaller membership churches. However, even in churches of varying size, the greater the number of social outreach programs, the more likely the growth in membership. The African American church has discovered that as it serves the community, it simultaneously draws individuals and families into its body.

A majority of the survey respondents (54 percent) strongly approved of "clergy in their church taking part in protests and marches on civil rights issues" (Figure 6.5). This is especially true

**Figure 6.4. Participation in Social Services/
Community Programs, 2000**

	Total	AME	CME	AMEZ	UMC
Food Needs	75%	80%	68%	84%	84%
Cash Assistance	86%	84%	84%	92%	87%
Thrift Store	52%	53%	45%	66%	57%
Elderly Help	36%	39%	36%	50%	41%
Counseling	66%	63%	50%	66%	59%
Substance Abuse	52%	51%	43%	66%	52%
Youth Programs	92%	94%	89%	94%	90%
Tutoring	65%	67%	60%	66%	70%
Voter Help	76%	86%	78%	86%	73%
Social Advocacy	45%	56%	43%	62%	63%
Employment	46%	46%	34%	54%	40%
Health	62%	69%	56%	74%	76%
Sr. Citizen Programs	57%	63%	58%	68%	67%
Prison Ministry	62%	56%	55%	66%	42%
Credit Unions	6%	9%	7%	6%	6%
Computer Training	42%	46%	38%	41%	52%

for large congregations in general (61 percent strongly agree), as well as African Methodist Episcopal (72 percent), Christian Methodist Episcopal (65 percent), African Methodist Episcopal Zion (72 percent), Black United Methodist (73 percent), and Black Presbyterians (73 percent) in particular. The Church of God in Christ pastors expressed much less support (35 percent) for these kinds of activities. A majority of all clergy interviewed (64 percent) strongly approved of churches expressing their views on day-to-day social and political issues.

On Being the Church in the World

The responsibility of the Church is not only to think about itself within the clichéd "four walls," but also to be aware of its 'hood and also to consider its life in the 'hood against what goes on in the

**Figure 6.4. Participation in Social Services/
Community Programs, 2000 (continued)**

	Baptist	COGIC	Presbyterian
Food Needs	76%	71%	78%
Cash Assistance	89%	82%	84%
Thrift Store	51%	51%	50%
Elderly Help	38%	29%	34%
Counseling	70%	64%	56%
Substance Abuse	52%	52%	39%
Youth Programs	93%	90%	89%
Tutoring	68%	59%	78%
Voter Help	79%	64%	74%
Social Advocacy	47%	32%	56%
Employment	47%	47%	37%
Health	66%	51%	70%
Sr. Citizen Programs	62%	42%	60%
Prison Ministry	66%	65%	35%
Credit Unions	5%	7%	6%
Computer Training	7%	33%	50%

**Figure 6.5. Black Church Practices Regarding Civil Rights
Activities and Social/Political Issues, by Percentage of
Pastoral Leaders Approving**

	Clergy Taking Part in Protest March on Civil Rights	Churches Expressing Their Views on Day-to-Day Social and Political Issues
Total Sample	54%	64%
Baptist	55%	64%
COGIC	35%	54%
AME	72%	73%
CME	65%	71%
AMEZ	72%	74%
UMC	73%	75%
Presbyterian	73%	77%

world beyond the 'hood. Our thinking must be about the wholeness and interdependence of life in this one world. Our challenge
is to identify common trends, problems, and responses and examine how they affect our understanding of the nature and mission
of the Church.

We offer three biblical passages for consideration, images that
describe the Church, and particularly the Church in the world.

1. The People of God (Exod. 19:5–6; Deut. 7:6–8; 1 Pet. 2:4–10)

The Church belongs to God's ancient purpose expressed in the
call to Israel. As Israel was redeemed from slavery and became
the people of God, all who come to Christ receive mercy and new
life and become part of the new people of God. There are two
functions that characterize this people: worship and witness. Both
functions are carried out by the whole people (*laos,* or laity) of
God, and not just by a special group alone. Early in its life, however, the distinctions of the Greco-Roman world crept into the life
of the Church. In the civil order there were distinctions between
the *kléros* (the clergy, the officials) and the laity (everybody else,
those who held no offices). The Church as the whole people of
God is evangelistic by its very nature. It must be the bearer of
good news — not only by *word,* but also in *deed,* in lifestyle.

2. The Body of Christ (Rom. 12:1–8; 1 Cor. 6:15–20; 11:23–26; 12:13–27)

In a profound sense the Church is Christ visible *in* and *for* the
world. The Body of Christ was given for the world. In that act of
self-giving, sealed by his death and resurrection, there came into
being the new community, the Body of Christ, commissioned to
carry out Christ's ministry to the world. In real terms, this means
that each of us embodies this ministry. It means that each of us

must offer up our body to God in worship and service. But each member, or each group of members, acts not by itself, but always as part of the whole Body. Cooperation among Christians and churches is not optional; it is demanded by the very nature and calling of the Church.

3. *The Commissioned Church (John 20:19–23; Luke 24:36–53)*

Whatever we say about the Church derives from the words and works of Jesus Christ himself. It derives more particularly from the resurrection event and the outpouring of the Holy Spirit — the Pentecostal event. The risen Christ is abroad and in God's world. The empowering Spirit is available to Christians and to the Church. The Church, which sometimes forgets these realities of our faith, tends to live behind closed doors, fearful of a hostile world. Such a Church is concerned mainly in self-preservation. But Christ breaks through to the Church with his risen presence. He commissions the Church to go out into the world. The Church is commissioned to proclaim the shattering and unique message that there is for-giveness with God, and that God through Jesus would always be present in the world with us. God goes before us, and we must learn to discern God's presence in the world. God accompanies us each step of the way. The mark of faith lies not in our desire to make sure that God is present with us, but in our willingness to keep company with God on the way. God is going to be there, but we must walk with God. That's faith. And finally, God will bring up the rear. And all of these promises God will keep to the "end of the age."

St. Mark's: Cleaning Up, Redeeming, and Adopting Its Community

The pastors at St. Mark's note that the church's approach to social activism has changed. Protests and picket lines are a thing of the past. Now the members of the congregation participate in activism through its mission programs. An example of this is the children's connection ministry for the children of incarcerated women. This daily program provides a safe, loving atmosphere and assistance for children with their homework assignments. St. Mark's is also engaged in community economic development. Although the majority of the members of the congregation no longer reside in the same neighborhood as the church, the senior pastor is committed to investing in the community. Many in the congregation wish that the new sanctuary had been built in another part of the city — away from the neighborhood known for gangs and drug dealers — and closer to their residential communities.

St. Mark's seeks to be the people of God for the community among whom its journey is set. The evidence of this is in its many ministries that touch the lives in their neighborhood. The associate pastor cited two examples: the In-Between Bible Study Class, initiated by the senior pastor when he noticed people clustering in groups around the church between services, and a tutorial program for children in the 'hood.

A General View of
Black Pastoral Leaders

Black Church pastoral leaders in general view their congregations as spiritually vital and alive. One characterization, used by a majority of clergy among all seven denominational groups considered in this study, is working for social justice. In fact when it came to moving beyond community service into social issue advocacy or community organizing, historically Black churches rate both issues more highly than all other faith groups (Figures 6.6 and 6.7).

Figure 6.6. Faith Communities and Advocacy for Justice, by Percentage of Congregations with Strong Programs

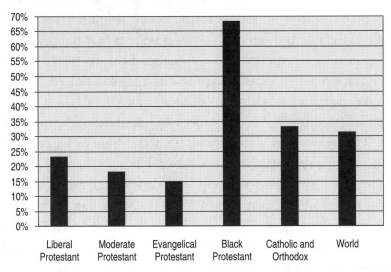

Source: Dudley and Roozen, *Faith Communities Today,* 49.

Figure 6.7. Faith Communities and Community Organizing, by Percentage of Congregations with Strong Programs

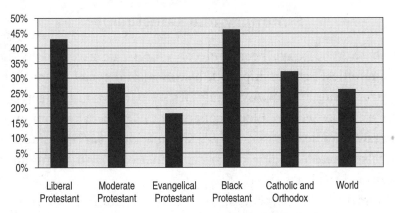

Source: Dudley and Roozen, *Faith Communities Today,* 49.

Challenges to the Future

We have been reporting and the FACT study confirms that Black congregations are responding to the needs of hidden and hurting people in their communities. The data suggests that Black churches will continue to respond. The times ahead call for proactive and creative approaches to address problems that will not go away, for example, new and subtle forms of racism and the AIDS pandemic, which is affecting the African American population disproportionately. The temptation is to retreat and do nothing or be persuaded by those who suggest that the Church has no relevance in these matters. Our ability to respond will depend on our earnest attempts to include all members in the tasks according to their gifts, skills, and talents. Equally important is the ability of leaders and congregations to discover where resources can be accessed, where networks can be joined, where alliances can be formed with those who are committed to the welfare of all persons. Finally, our ability to respond will rest not on the soundness of our analysis, though that is important, but on our willingness to risk our security on behalf of the insecurities of others.

Summary and Conclusion

Black churches have been and continue to be involved in their communities. Scholarship both historical and social scientific has illustrated this. The ICAM study of 141 parishes in thirteen communities focused on Black congregations that take community outreach and service seriously.[30] Our national survey of approximately nineteen hundred African American faith communities confirmed that fact.[31]

More than 90 percent of all the Black churches surveyed in this project indicated that they were involved in some community outreach programs. In fact, outreach ministries are more important to the historically Black Protestant churches than any other faith community. The majority of African American clergy are supportive of involvement in civil rights concerns as well as day-to-day social and political issues.

In our study African American pastors indicated that they were strong advocates for social justice and community organizing. No other faith community examined in the FACT project gave as strong an endorsement as the African American pastoral leaders.

7

RESOURCES IN BLACK CONGREGATIONAL LIFE

In their extremely useful book *Studying Congregations: A New Handbook,* Nancy Ammerman and her colleagues discuss congregational resources in several important ways. They argue that "all the raw materials of congregational life — human, economic and capital, spiritual, and reputational" — should be considered.[32] They suggest that both hard and countable resources as well as soft and relational ones must be included. This chapter will focus on both. Black churches have multiple resources in their religious and social settings. People, acts of commitment, financial holdings and expenditures, capital investments, physical and spatial gifts, as well as spiritual undergirding all contribute to the vast resource base of African American religiosity.

People Resources

The average number of members on the congregational rolls of all African American churches studied was approximately 500 (Figure 7.1). This number varies widely according to the denomination and represents an estimate only. Baptists reported having the highest average at 704, while Black Presbyterians had the lowest (194). The Church of God in Christ reported 255, African Methodist

Figure 7.1. Black Church Membership Estimates

Church	Average Reported Membership
Total Sample	500
Baptist	704
AME	516
UMC	430
CME	312
AMEZ	255
COGIC	255
Presbyterian	194

Episcopal 516, Christian Methodist Episcopal 312, African Methodist Episcopal Zion 255, and Black United Methodists 430. These numbers are estimates of the numbers on church membership rolls, not estimates of regular participation in each church.

In terms of church participation among the 1863 churches studied, pastors and senior lay leaders reported an average of 100 active adult members regularly participating in the religious life of their churches. Many churches have fewer active members, while some have significantly more. However, a majority of all churches (58 percent) reported that the number of their regularly participating adults increased 5 percent or more during 1995–2000. Only 8 percent of the churches reported that they had experienced a decline in participation. In a separate question asking about church attendance on a typical Sunday, the average attendance was reported to be 278. It was much higher for the Baptists and much lower for CME, AMEZ, COGIC, and Black Presbyterians. Thus in the total sample of the 1863 churches studied, the pastors reported that, on average, they had approximately 500 members, with 278 attending worship on a typical Sunday, and 100 adults who regularly participating in the religious life of their church. This underscores one reality of congregational life: there is a significant difference between being listed on the church roll and actively participating in regular church and community activities. It is important to recognize, however, that these churches possess great human capital. They have many persons involved in their churches and communities on a regular ongoing basis. The Black Church has always been and continues to be a religious and social institution with significant people power.

Chapter 2 highlighted the makeup of Black Church membership. Overall African American churches attract a strong diversity of individuals and families: younger people and old; families with minimal incomes and those with much greater financial resources; college graduates and those with less education. These persons give of their time and energy to their churches and their respective communities. They are the human capital of African American congregational life.

Assimilation

Black churches have learned to incorporate new members into their congregations. They add to their human capital as they assimilate new people into their fellowships. In fact, compared to most other faith groups, the historically Black Protestant churches reported a higher level of acceptance of new people (72 percent). Only some of the groups identified as world religions (Baha'is, Mormons, and Muslims) reported higher levels of assimilation.[33]

A strong majority of churches in the total sample of Black churches do well incorporating new persons into their life and fellowship. The effectiveness with which African American congregations assimilate new people and retain them as members is not related to region of the country or rural-urban location. Larger Black churches have the advantage in offering program diversity and worship experience. However, size is not very important; larger African American churches are only slightly more likely than smaller membership churches to incorporate new individuals easily. Generally speaking, Black congregations that demonstrate strong expressions of their heritage and are spiritually vital assimilate newcomers well.[34]

As we have seen, African American churches, compared to other faith groups, tend to assimilate their newcomers more easily. When Black denominational groups are compared within themselves, there are differences — especially among Black United Methodists and Black Presbyterians, who report that their ease of assimilating new members is not as strong as the other black Protestant faith groups (see Figure 3.3, p. 37). Of some concern is the fact that relatively few clergy in any of the denominations felt that the statement "new members are easily assimilated into the life of your congregation" described their church very well (39 percent of the pastors were a "5" on a five-point scale). Among the six characteristics tested, this statement received the lowest score on the five-point scale. While the Black Presbyterian and Black United Methodists were very low, the Church of God in Christ leaders had a much stronger assessment of their assimilation process (45 percent with "5"; see Figure 3.6, p. 39).

Surprisingly, few significant differences emerged based on the sizes of the congregation in terms of ease of incorporation. Approximately 39 percent of the pastors in small, medium, and large churches reported that new members were easily assimilated. Female pastors were somewhat more positive than male pastors: 37 percent of the men said this statement described their church very well as compared to 47 percent of the women.

Financial Resources

Approximately two-thirds of the clergy members contacted in this study felt that their congregation's financial health was currently

**Figure 7.2. Financial Health among Black Congregations,
by Percentage of Congregations**

	Good	Tight	Difficult
Total Sample	64%	33%	3%
Baptist	73%	24%	3%
COGIC	58%	39%	3%
AME	61%	36%	3%
CME	63%	32%	5%
AMEZ	67%	29%	4%
UMC	64%	32%	4%
Presbyterian	58%	42%	0%

"good" (64 percent), while 33 percent felt that it was tight (Figure 7.2). Only 3 percent among the entire sample of Black churches indicated that their church was in serious financial difficulty. Larger Black churches were more likely to report being in good financial health than smaller membership churches. Similarly, congregations that had grown 5 percent or more since 1995 were more likely to demonstrate good financial health. Even among the growing churches, however, the larger churches still had an advantage.

The financial health of a Black church depends on its size and financial resources. Churches with a large proportion of adult members with family incomes less that $20,000 a year are significantly less likely to be financially stable than churches with adults with higher incomes. As we might expect, the churches in the best financial health are clearly the larger churches with relatively few low-income families.

Overall, the financial health of the congregations examined appeared to be getting stronger. When asked to describe their churches' financial health in 1995, only 49 percent said that it was good, while in the year 2000 64 percent reported good financial health.

Nearly all the pastors (95 percent) reported that at least some of their members tithe. Pastors were then asked about the percentage of tithers in their congregation. The average was 45 percent. Specifically, 3 percent of the church leaders reported that less than 5 percent of their congregations tithed while 11 percent reported that between 5 and 10 percent did so. Another 16 percent reported that between 11 to 25 percent of the members tithed, while 19 percent reported 26–49 percent. Finally, 41 percent of the respondents indicated that 50 percent or more were tithers in their congregation. A total of 10 percent were not certain of the proportion of tithers in their parishes. Again, it is important to remember that these are estimates only.

Estimates or not, Black churches generate significant levels of giving among their people. Many individuals and families attempt to give 10 percent of their gross or net income. In the recent study conducted by the Institute of Church Administration and Management (ICAM) at the Interdenominational Theological Center, it was reported that tithing was a common practice among the majority (65 percent) of the church members studied. While this study examined only a total of 141 churches in thirteen different settings across the United States, it did highlight the importance of African American church members giving through the local and national churches. Black congregants support their churches and demonstrate a strong commitment to sharing their financial resources.[35]

The Use of Space in Facilities

Project 2000 did not gather a great deal of information on questions regarding facilities and use of space. However, the overall FACT study did so, addressing such matters as surplus educational

**Figure 7.3. Churches Reporting Surplus Educational Space,
Percentage by Location**

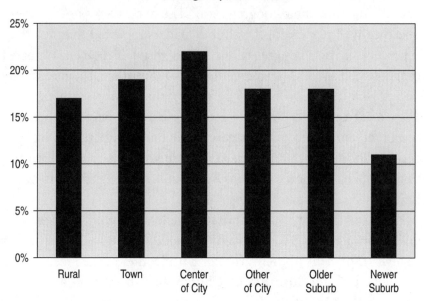

Source: Dudley and Roozen, *Faith Communities Today,* 54.

space and parking problems. Dudley and Roozen reported that many congregations outside the suburban locations indicated that they had more space than they needed (Figure 7.3).

> Fortunately, many of the congregations with additional or unused room are located in communities of greatest need for human services in rural and central city settings. They are uniquely situated to respond with space and facilities to provide faith-based social ministries to strengthen their communities, where no other such building may be available.[36]

If we consider that the Black Church is heavily concentrated in urban settings, particularly center-city locations, this overall

**Figure 7.4. Congregations Needing More Parking,
Percentage by Location**

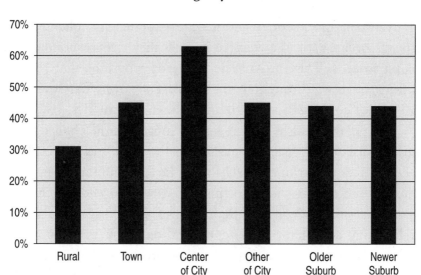

Source: Dudley and Roozen, *Faith Communities Today*, 55.

finding suggests that African American congregations have space resources that are not always being used. Many of them are using their resources productively, as we saw in chapter 6, but more can be done. The point here is that spatial resources are available in African American congregational settings.

The need for additional parking is another resource issue (Figure 7.4). Dudley and Roozen also discovered that the greatest need for parking space is in the inner city.[37] Again, many Black churches reside in the heart of our American urban areas. Like some other faith groups who have not abandoned the urban dwellers of the central city, they desperately need additional parking for their members and visitors.

Growth, Expansion, and Parking: Issues for the Future

Many urban Black congregations are experiencing phenomenal growth because of the way in which they are responding to people's needs. They provide a variety of programs that require parking facilities throughout the week. They are what some call full-service congregations with a full range of activities.

Growing and healthy congregations must face the challenges of parking just as they face other demands for space and its use. They need to think of parking in relation to the total number of persons who use the facilities and not just those who attend the Sunday worship services. Kennon Callahan offers some sage counsel for preliminary consideration as congregations look to their future and the challenges of parking. "There is direct correlation between three elements: parking, worship attendance, and giving. To discover the annual giving value of each parking space, divide the total number of parking spaces into the total giving to all causes for the most recent year."[38]

In our Project 2000, focused exclusively on African American congregations, 13 percent of the clergy respondents reported that other congregations shared their church buildings. Church of God in Christ pastors were most likely to report this (17 percent), while African Methodist Episcopal Zion clergy were least likely to report dual usage (8 percent). Churches in the East and West were more likely than those in the South and Midwest to report that their churches were used by other congregations. Surprisingly, no differences emerged according to whether the church was located in an urban, suburban, or rural setting.

Among the 13 percent of pastors who reported dual use of their churches, most indicated that the other congregation that used the churches conducted their worship services in English (73 percent) while 22 percent reported that the other services were in Spanish. Regional differences were clearly found in response to these questions. Half of the pastors in the West reported that the other congregations using the building conducted their worship services in Spanish, while only 12 percent in the East reported this.

Black Church Philanthropy

Our current research about social and political outreach should not surprise anyone who has at least an elementary level of awareness concerning the philanthropic spirit of the Black religious community. This outpouring of service can be seen in both Christian contexts and Muslim. This outreach has been found to be fairly consistent in rural, urban, and suburban settings, in small membership gatherings as well as so-called megachurches. The *Journal of the Interdenominational Theological Center*, edited by Joseph E. Troutman and Reta L. Bigham, details this reality.[39]

Neither the Black religious community in general, nor the widely varied Black congregations and masjids in particular, are perfect in social and religious behavior or uniformly consistent in all beliefs. However, a cooperative collectivism and a deep sense of community and self-worth based on helping others help to explain the generosity of African American people.

In her book *Survival of the Black Family* Sue Jewell contends that no formal institutional support systems existed within the African American community for a significant period of time. Instead "informal social-systems, led by the Black church" have "espoused the importance of sharing and caring among Black families" and represent a form of cooperative collectivism that runs contrary to North American competitive individualism.[40] Especially in the years immediately following slavery, African American families had to depend on one another to survive. Basic goods such as food, shelter, and clothing often came through "informal neighbor networks,"[41] which reinforced a cooperative collectivism among African Americans.

The Black Church and its self-help tradition was the primary social institution in the African American community that fostered an ongoing mutuality and cooperativeness. As Lincoln and Mamiya explain, mutual aid societies and churches were "among the first social institutions created by black people" and they existed in a symbiotic relationship.[42] They often spawned one another, but both existed for the purpose of helping individuals and families in the larger African American community help themselves. They fostered schools, job training programs, credit unions, and other related economic and educational institutions to enable African American people to survive — not as isolated selves but as a whole people. They encouraged sharing and mutual responsibility. The mutual aid societies or fraternal orders and their auxiliaries "espoused philosophical issues inextricably related to the religious doctrine of the Black church, such as mutual dependence, collective responsibility, and cooperation."[43] Thus formal and informal institutions were created and provided African American women and men necessary social-support systems from the time of slavery to the present.

Jewell argues that certain forms of U.S. social policy have begun to diminish the sense of community. Yet, she and others contend, a cooperative collectivism has existed in the past and still persists even today within the African American community:

Competitive individualism as a value system had greater applicability to white families with a male head, since he was the most likely family member to be involved in competition in the labor force. Hence, resources were initially acquired and mediated by the male head of the household and later shared with members of his nuclear family. Because black two-parent families, for the most part, have been characterized by dual wage earners, and extended, augmented, and subfamilies, sharing and merging resources took precedence over a monopoly of resources by any one family member. In effect, structural barriers resulted in black families subscribing to cooperative collectivism for the purpose of survival and advancement.[44]

While such communal values may have been a historical necessity for the African American family and larger community, today the entire nation could benefit from a value system grounded in a cooperative spirit and collective sense of relatedness, as modeled in the Black religious community. North American men and women need to discover alternatives to the rampant and often destructive individualism that the majority culture perpetuates. The African American community and especially the Black Church, which lies at its center, models that alternative.

Cooperative collectivism helps to nurture a sense of community and connectedness. It prompts a sense of a greater whole that may include the individual self, but certainly transcends that self. This sense of community is an essential quality of the Black religious experience. It is a quality that originated in African culture and carries over today beyond indigenous African society.

John Mbiti underscores that throughout traditional African cultures there was a deep sense of community. Individuals were born into a tribe and family but saw themselves as more than an individual self or creature. They were part of a larger whole — the community. Persons became who they were in community and not as distinct from it.

In traditional life, the individual does not and cannot exist alone except corporately. He owes his existence to other people, including those of past generations and his contemporaries. He is simply part of the whole. The community must therefore make, create or produce the individual; for the individual depends on that corporate group. Physical birth is not enough: the child must go through rites of incorporation so that it becomes fully integrated into the entire society. The rites continue throughout the physical life of person, during which the individual passes from one stage of corporate existence to another. The final stage incorporated the individual into the wider family of both the dead and the living.[45]

Mbiti affirms that this understanding of the human creature is profoundly religious in traditional African culture. God made the first human being and now humans produce others, but others who become corporate or social beings. This according to Mbiti is a "deeply religious transaction."

Only in terms of other people does the individual become conscious of his own being, his own duties, his privileges and responsibilities towards other people. When he suffers, he does not suffer alone but with the corporate group; when he rejoices, he rejoices not alone but with his relatives dead or living. When he gets married, he is not alone, neither does the wife "belong" to him alone. So also the children belong to the corporate body of kinsmen, even if they bear only their father's name. Whatever happens to the individual happens to the whole group, and whatever happens to the whole group happens to the individual. The individual can only say: "I am, because we are; and since we are, therefore I am." This is a cardinal point in the understanding of the African view of man.[46]

It is a view of humankind that is consistent with an underlying principle of Christian experience, namely, that members of the

Body of Christ belong to one another. Ephesians 4:25b (NRSV) proposes that this is the nature of the Christian community, "for we are members of one another." The letter to the church at Corinth makes the same point. "If one member suffers, all suffer together with it; if one member is honored, all rejoice together with it" (1 Cor. 12:26 NRSV). The Black religious community has found a way to maintain this fundamental African and early Christian belief system. The basic community and those community ties, which exist among its individual members, are of primary importance. People are connected to one another within the framework of the larger community. Individual contractual relations are important but experienced within a deeper sense of community. Communal bonds among Black religionists are quite strong. These socioreligious group ties are a significant indicator of the importance of community in the African American context. According to Roof and McKinney,

> Black Protestants attend worship services more than any other group except white conservative Protestants; 56 percent are regular attendees and 25 percent are occasional attendees.... Generally blacks have a high level of denominational commitment, much higher in fact than most other groups. With respect to membership in a church group — perhaps the best measure of communal bonds — they exceed all the other [church] families. They are the only [religious body or] family for which more than one-half claim involvement in a church group. Strong bonds to church and community have served to buffer somewhat the trends toward greater religious individualism dominant in the society.[47]

Another important aspect of the Black religious community is the value placed on helping others. Unlike much of contemporary American culture, which bases value and self-worth on material acquisition, the Black religious community places value and self worth on the helping of others. Sharing with others, giving to those who are needy has been and continues to be of great significance to African American people. The worth of individuals is based not so much on how much they have amassed economically as on how much they share with others.

Some scholars argue that this tendency to help and share with others dates back to the time of the slavery. It was a terrible and dehumanizing period of history that forced slave men and women to look solely at themselves and their slave brothers and sisters for support:

> Mothers relied on older relatives or neighbors in the slave quarters to watch the children while they spent the day in the fields. During illness, injury, and death the slaves learned to take care of each other and depend on one another because there was no one else. When death or sale took the parents of young children, the children were raised and cared for by other slaves, irrespective of kinship or lack of it.[48]

When a person chooses to share material possessions with others, the status and esteem of the giver greatly increases. The Black Church places less emphasis on individual accumulation and greater value on shared resources.[49]

Christian Community as Household of God

As we have seen, one of the New Testament descriptions of the Christian community is "household of God" (Eph. 2:19). The concept of the Church as the household of God reflects a pattern of thought and expression familiar to the Hebrews. Household or family would be natural ways of thinking of people and peoples.

Through Abraham "all the families of the earth shall bless themselves" (Gen. 12:3; 28:14). The concepts of the Fatherhood of God and life in the Church as family life are a part of the understanding of the Church as the household of God. But God is the Father of Jesus Christ and God is "our Father" only because we are in Christ and because of our new relationship to Jesus Christ. Paul describes this as "adoption" (Rom. 8:15, 23; 9:4; Gal. 4:5; Eph. 1:5). It is through the Holy Spirit that we are permitted to address God as *Abba,* Father.

One of the important consequences for our understanding of life in the Church as household of God is the acknowledgment of the interrelationship among persons within that household. The life to be lived is a family life, in which both the riches and the disciplines of Christian living are to be experienced. In the Old Testament the term for a member of a Hebrew community is "neighbor" or "kinsman" (Lev. 19:16–18). The whole of Israel is family, and all Israelites are brothers and sisters (Exod. 2:11; Lev. 10:6; Jer. 34:14). In the New Testament, the term "brother" came to be used for members of the Christian community and brotherly love the accepted standard of Christian virtue (Rom. 12:10; 1 Thess. 4:9; 1 Pet. 1:22). As we take our place within the Church, we must accept others as those whom we cannot reject. We cannot pick and choose our brothers and sisters. Because it is God who through the Holy Spirit calls us into the family relationship, we may not erect barriers that divide those who feel that they belong from those who are not yet God's people.

According to Robert Staples, African Americans maintain certain values that often differ from the value orientation of European Americans. The mutual aid one offers is one such example. "While Anglo-Saxon norms dictate individualism and competitivism, Blacks tend to believe that they should help anyone in need. They have faith in the spirit of cooperation rather than competition. This value is reflected in their views on poverty, welfare and the ill-fed, and their exchange network."[50]

Staples argues that money in the African American community is seen as a means to further communalism and not necessarily accumulated. "How money is used is more important than its acquisition. Property is a collective asset, not an individual one."[51] Thus one's sense of self and status within the community stems more from personal qualities such as courtesy, compassion and the helping of others.

Summary and Conclusion

African American people are characterized by multiple resources in and beyond their local church communities. They include both "hard," countable resources, as well as "soft," relational ones.

The people themselves are invaluable resources. They experience God and God's people, they share their stories and the story of Jesus, and they actively pray and intentionally act in their homes, churches, and communities.

Our study of African American congregational life found that the average membership of all Black churches surveyed is five hundred. Baptist churches claim to have somewhat larger overall memberships, while Black Presbyterians reported a much smaller total, approximately 194.

Incorporating new members into the various Black churches was reported as somewhat easier to accomplish than in almost every other faith community — liberal Protestant, moderate Protestant, evangelical Protestant, Catholic, and Orthodox.

Most respondents in our survey affirmed that their churches were in strong financial health. In fact almost two-thirds (64 percent) of all Black congregations indicated that they were in "good financial health." While many of the African American congregations confirmed that finances were tight (33 percent), only a few indicated that money was a major problem (3 percent).

Spiritually, things look good in Black congregational life at the turn of the century. The pastors or their assistants who responded to our inquiry manifested a strong spiritual base. There is an important spiritual dimension to the way that African Americans describe their churches and the content of sermons preached.

We discovered that Black churches might have space available in the heart of our cities, which could be better utilized in the future. Parking is a major problem for Black Church congregants and may continue to be the case.

8

LEADERSHIP IN BLACK CONGREGATIONS

The responsibilities of Christian leadership are clear. Leaders arise from the community and are responsible to the community as bearers of the holy, a means by which the community is led into relationship with God. Leaders must also use the gifts with which they have been endowed to assure that the tasks of the community are accomplished. At a deeper level, pastoral leadership derives from God and is sustained through relationship with God. Ministry is neither an office, nor a career, but rather a vocation and a calling. And more importantly, our work does not separate us from others. As Moffatt suggests in his commentary on Hebrews 5:2, "The *àrchiereús* — the high priest — is able to deal gently with the erring People whom he represents, since he shares their *àsthéneia,* their common infirmity, or liability to temptation" — their weakness and frailty.[52] These are sobering thoughts when we would presume to judge others. We are bound up with our fellow human beings in the bundle of life. Leaders who make the inward journey both to their shadows and lights can take us beyond ourselves into a needy and hurting world.

The role of pastoral leader is to free up the laity for greater responsibilities. "The clergy are being asked to identify, enlist, nurture, disciple, train, place, support, and resource teams of lay volunteers who will do the work.... This may also be the most demanding role for ministers in terms of vision, competence, creativity, leadership, dedication, strategy formulation, hard work, long hours, faithfulness, and skill in interpersonal relationships."[53]

Leaders "don't make plans, they don't solve problems; they don't even organize people. What leaders really do is prepare organizations for change and help them cope as they go through it."[54] Leadership is the most effective way to intervene in an organization and shift its goals. The challenge that confronts a good leader is to help people into new ways of thinking and understanding, accepting new configurations, behaving in new and different ways, and producing new results.

The Work of the Laity: The People of God in the Congregation

Henry Henson came as a new pastor to Shady Grove and refused to recognize that he had in his congregation persons with varieties of gifts for the common task. The ministry belongs to the whole people of God and is not the pastor's private possession. Yet the language pastors use suggests that as they speak of "my church" and "how many souls they got for the kingdom."

In one of the finance meetings at Shady Grove, Pastor Henson silenced Sister Jessie Thomas as she attempted to contribute to the discussion on the church's budget. She tried to make sure that responsible use was being made of the church's resources. Jessie Thomas was director of budget and management in city government, and Pastor Henson had appointed her to the church finance committee, but now he was dismissing what she had to say, declaring that he was in charge and that his actions were not to be questioned. Regrettably, because of the pastor's attitude, Sister Jessie withdrew from the committee and from membership in that congregation. We need to find ways not only for identifying and managing the varied gifts of members, but also affirming them as they make those gifts available in the congregation. To this end, pastoral leaders are challenged to affirm and empower persons to use their gifts for the benefit of the common ministry entrusted to the congregation.

Ministry belongs to the whole People of God (*laos,* or laity). It is not the private possession of the pastor or minister. The whole tenor of Paul's argument in Ephesians 4:7–16 reminds us that the gifts that we have are part of Christ's endowment. The Greek word *dowrea* has many interesting ideas surrounding it. Our English word *dowry,* which has its roots in Medieval English, is quite similar in concept. In other cultures, including some African cultures, the *dowry* is the money, goods, or estate that a woman brings to her husband in marriage.

God has gifted us within the community of faith to accomplish the different tasks of the ministry. We may not mature in the faith apart from our engagement in the work that God has for us through the congregation. The pastoral leader's share in that ministry is to affirm persons within the community of faith and enable persons to discern and use those gifts for ministry of the whole people of God through that congregation.

The Church is not the only organization in the society that uses volunteers to fulfill its mission or purpose. According to Peter Drucker, "Few people are aware that the nonprofit sector is by far America's largest employer. Every other adult — a total of 80 million people — works as a volunteer, giving on average nearly five hours each to one or several nonprofit organizations. This is equal to 10 million full-time jobs.... But more and more volunteers are becoming 'unpaid staff' taking over the professional and managerial tasks in their organizations."[55]

What we learn from nonprofits is that clarity of purpose or mission enables the organization not only to focus on action, but also to develop strategies for attaining goals set by the organization. This is echoed by findings from the FACT study of religious life in the United States. "Congregations with a clear sense of purpose feel vital and alive.... Vital purposeful congregations have a more positive assessment about their future. Such optimism occurs most often in historically Black churches, and significantly less often in Moderate Protestant congregations. Not surprisingly, the confidence of congregations in their future is closely tied to their ability to attract and mobilize the energies of their youth."[56]

A clearly defined mission will energize the commitment of persons as they share their ideas for the achievement of established goals. Meaningful engagement always has the potential to maximize the productivity of those who volunteer their time and energies. Churches must find creative ways to recognize and celebrate the contributions of those who invest themselves and share their gifts, talents, and skills in furthering the mission of their local congregations.

Building a Team for Ministry

An Akan proverb states, "If you say you know everything, you will sleep in the hallway of fools." No one of us has all that it takes to work for God. We need others and others need us. The days of the pastoral leader who has all the ideas, makes all the decisions, can do all that needs to be done are past. Perhaps, they never were. The recognition of this reality has come home sharply to those who lead congregations. There has been a paradigm shift in the leadership of congregations. Pastors must be open to, nurture, and prepare persons for shared leadership, to become partners in ministry.

As pastors help persons to invest in themselves and believe in their potential, they will move away from doing things *to* people and toward doing things *with* people. People readily submit to working with a leader who empowers others. When persons participate in shaping the work to be done, they can evaluate their progress, revise their plans, making adjustments where necessary and certainly celebrate achievements. A pastoral leader, who inspires, encourages and supports persons as they fulfill their share of the ministry, will earn the trust and respect that he or she anticipates from the congregation

On Leadership and Management

Leadership and management are two different skills. Sometimes they may reside in one person. When they do not, they need to be recognized as complementary. Both are needed to assist the congregation to do its work. One way to talk about the differences between leadership and management is to recognize how we relate to people. We show caring and quality leadership as we demonstrate a greater concern for building people rather than using them.

> Leadership is different from management....It has nothing to do with charisma or other exotic personality traits. It is not the province of a chosen few. Nor is leadership better than management or a replacement of it. Rather leadership and management are two distinctive and complementary systems of action. Each has its own function and characteristic activities. Both are necessary for success in an increasingly complex and volatile business environment.[57]

Pastoral leaders who are more than managers support persons as they are assigned to the tasks in the congregation. They seek to match the gifts of the members to the assignments needed to get the jobs done. As the congregation seeks to fulfill its mission, they delegate others for participation in the action. They find ways to listen carefully as persons share their ideas so that they might understand well the contributions that others are willing to make. They seize opportunities to affirm persons who have committed themselves to participate in achieving the goals of the organization. In these and other ways they demonstrate the difference between leadership and management.

Growing Leaders from within the Community of Faith

One concern that faces African American congregations is recruiting and nurturing pastoral leaders. A manifestation that the faith has taken root among a people is the emergence from the ranks of leaders they can identify and call their own. This occurs as congregations create conditions of nurture in faith development and the kind of spiritual environment in which persons can hear and discern the call of God. We each tell our own story. Paul reminds the Corinthians to recall the kinds of persons they were when God called them:

> Not many were wise by human standards; not many were powerful, not many were of noble birth. But God chose what is foolish in the world to shame the wise; God chose what is weak in the world to shame the strong; God chose what is low and despised in the world, the things that are not, to reduce to nothing things that are, so that no one might boast in the presence of God. He is the source of your life in Christ Jesus, who has become for us wisdom from God, and righteousness and sanctification and redemption, in order that, as it is written, "Let the one who boasts boast in the Lord." (1 Cor. 1:26–31).

It is in this context of nurture in the community of faith that persons can be open to discern the claim of God on their lives and to hear a call to ministry.

As we work with our own congregation or one with which we may be affiliated, we need to be open to cultivating and nurturing persons for their roles as disciples. God will use the Holy Spirit in the congregation to renew and resource the Church for building up the Body of Christ and bringing the reign of God nearer. "Thy kingdom come" is the prayer that Jesus taught. But the coming of the kingdom is not automatic. It requires the collaboration of human beings. Our participation includes providing assistance, always being in solidarity with others, and working constantly for the liberation of the oppressed. "Truly I tell you, just as you did it to one of the least of these who are members of my family, you did it to me" (Matt. 25:40, 45).

"If It Wasn't for Women...": Realities That Should Be Recognized

Women have continued in every available forum to raise their voices to claim legitimate leadership roles in the Church. Their claim has been articulate, impassioned, and insistent. But their leadership roles are still limited in many African American congregations. The lack of access to the pulpit is only one manifestation of the problem. They are grudgingly placed on deacon and trustee boards as members. Their presence is carefully limited and managed so that election to leadership as chairperson is rare. An even greater and more pressing concern is the affirmation and acceptance of women in pastoral leadership. Yet it is only as churches, and more particularly African American denominations, permit honest and open discussion at every level that women's potential for growth will be realized.

In such a discussion, there is a need to go beyond the old and tired arguments: that God does not call women to preach or lead congregations, that a woman could be an evangelist but not a pastor. The educational approach would seek to change the attitudes of persons, even some women, so that they are liberated to affirm that God's gifts are not gender assigned and limited to men. This needs to be a continuing educational experience in which the contributions that women have made and can make will be affirmed and redound to the enrichment of the life of all persons in the congregations.

•

When Pastor McClain came to Mount Nebo, he sensed the walls of traditionalism, but he felt that these walls did not need to be torn down; rather, they could be reconstructed. He established a twelve-week Bible study and teaching session. Persons were invited to talk about their fears and inhibitions concerning what up till that time had been mentioned only in muted conversations. An objective in the dialogue was attitudinal and behavioral change in all persons in the congregation — both men and women. An anticipated outcome was new and positive influences in social relations and the practices of ministry in congregation and community.

As a result of these meetings and the discussions that Pastor McClain initiated, women in ministry have been embraced and the by-laws of the church have been rewritten to reflect this commitment to women in ministry. The congregation affirms that there is a place for women in ministry at all levels and supports three women from the congregation who are now in seminary. The groundwork was being laid to qualify these persons for ministry and to prepare them for pastoral leadership roles.

Cheryl Townsend Gilkes contends, as the title of her book implies, that " 'if it wasn't for the women" the Black community would not have had the churches and other organizations that have

Figure 8.1. Total Sample of Black Churches: Educational Level of Pastoral Leadership

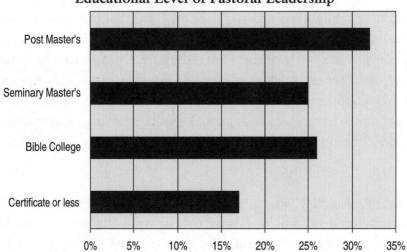

fostered the psychic and material survival of individuals and that have mobilized the constituencies that have produced change and progress."[58] The issue is one that African American denominations can no longer treat casually and tentatively. Delores Carpenter's *A Time for Honor* calls us to recognize and honor clergywomen who are eminently qualified for all aspects of leadership and ministry in churches.[59] She has carefully documented claims that cannot be denied. Denominations must therefore address with seriousness and creativity the issue of women in pastoral leadership. The gifts, talents, skills, and dedication that women have to offer can only continue to enhance the health and vitality of congregational life.

Pastor's Age, Gender, Education, Employment, and Attitudes

The average age of the pastors of the congregations interviewed was fifty-five and most (96 percent) were male. Overall, the highest

Figure 8.2. Black Denominational Groups:
Educational Level of Pastoral Leadership

	Certificate or Less	Bible College	Seminary Master's	Post-Master's
Total	17%	26%	25%	32%
Baptist	10%	28%	29%	33%
COGIC	36%	37%	12%	15%
AME	4%	17%	33%	46%
CME	22%	28%	26%	24%
AMEZ	9%	17%	32%	42%
UMC	1%	9%	32%	58%
Presbyterian	6%	3%	28%	63%

level of ministerial education for pastors interviewed was a post-master of divinity program or degree for 32 percent, seminary degree for 25 percent, and Bible college or some seminary for 26 percent. Only 4 percent reported an apprenticeship, 3 percent a certificate or correspondence program, and 9 percent reported none (Figure 8.1).

Pastors of Black Presbyterian and United Methodist churches were more likely than pastors of the other five denominations to have a post-master of divinity degree or doctor of ministry degree (Figure 8.2). Church of God in Christ pastors were the least likely to report advanced levels of formal ministerial training.

There was no direct relationship between levels of education and whether pastors reported their congregations as being spiritually vital, helping members deepen their relationship to God, being excited about the future, assimilating new comers, or working for social justice. However, the more education clergypersons have, the more likely they were to pastor larger congregations.

Approximately three-quarters of the pastors of the congregations interviewed were paid (full or part-time), while 25 percent were volunteers. Church of God in Christ churches were more

**Figure 8.3. Average Age of Leaders
among Different Faith Communities**

Liberal Protestant	52
Moderate Protestant	51
Evangelical Protestant	49
Historically Black Protestant	55
Catholic and Orthodox	56
World Groups	49

Source: Dudley and Roozen, *Faith Communities Today,* 65.

evenly divided between those who had a paid position (approx-imately 50 percent) and those who had volunteer pastors (50 percent). In a separate question, the survey found that a total of three-quarters of the pastors worked full time, while 13 percent worked full time as a pastor but supplemented their income by outside employment; 9 percent were part-time pastors. A total of 8 percent of clergy reported that they served more than one church.

The average age of the pastors in this study as compared to the spiritual leaders of other faith groups is significant (Figure 8.3). The Catholic and Orthodox religious communities and historically Black Protestant groups have the oldest religious leaders, and an average age of fifty-six and fifty-five respectively.

A majority of clergypersons strongly approved of "clergy in their churches taking part in protests and marches on civil rights issues" (54 percent) (Figure 8.4). This is especially true for large congregations (61 percent strongly approve). The African Meth-odist Episcopal (72 percent), Christian Methodist Episcopal (65 percent), African Methodist Episcopal Zion (72 percent), Black United Methodist (73 percent), and Black Presbyterian (73 per-cent) churches also strongly approve. A majority (64 percent) of all clergy interviewed strongly approved of churches expressing their views on day-to-day social and political issues.

Figure 8.4. Strong Approval of Church Practices among African American Denominational Groups

	Clergy involved in protest or civil rights	Churches expressing views on social and political issues	Women pastoring a church
Total	54%	64%	40%
Baptist	55%	64%	27%
COGIC	35%	54%	22%
AME	72%	73%	77%
CME	65%	71%	75%
AMEZ	72%	74%	78%
UMC	73%	75%	88%
Presbyterian	73%	77%	85%

The issue that reflected the widest divergence among the denominations was that of women pastors. Overall, 40 percent of all the clergy interviewed in this study approved of a woman serving as a pastor of a church. In the United Methodist (88 percent), Presbyterian (85 percent), African Methodist Episcopal Zion (78 percent), African Methodist Episcopal (77 percent), and Christian Methodist Episcopal churches (75 percent) the approval rating was quite high. However, only 27 percent of the Baptists and 22 percent of the Church of God in Christ pastors felt the same way. Women as pastors are not universally accepted in the African American religious setting.

Conflict, Growth, and Vitality

Dealing with conflict in the local church takes a special kind of leadership. While only 17 percent of the pastors or senior lay leaders who responded to the survey reported any level of major disagreement over the previous five years (1996–2000), a few specific issues did emerge. For example, money or finance-related concerns (for 19 percent of the respondents), general decision making (9 percent), and worship style (5 percent) were identified.

Conflict arises when we seek to make choices. As individuals, we face conflicts when we must make the choice to be one place or another. At the Church of the Redeemer an intergroup conflict was created by legitimate and competing claims between the women's auxiliary and the youth fellowship. Conflict will always be present where persons gather in community. We have different ways of looking at things. We bring to any circumstance the persons we are, with our knowledge, our experiences, and our beliefs.

Our life together in congregations mirrors our life in other encounters, and conflict is part of our common life. We begin to deal with it as we recognize that we have differences. How we deal with it and what use we make of it will determine the quality of our ongoing life together. Church groups and leaders tend to handle conflict poorly. Persons harbor resentments, sometimes holding on to unpleasant encounters for years. They are unwilling to let go and be reconciled. The beginning of the process to resolve conflict is the willingness to let go, which opens the way for forgiveness.

The issues of conflict, growth, and vitality are interrelated. Congregations that are willing to recognize conflict and enable the parties to deal with the issues have the capacity for vitality and growth. This is an opportunity where we can utilize the human relations skills of members trained in conflict resolution to serve as internal facilitators in the process. If the situation is so grave that it cannot be dealt with internally, it may be necessary to engage the services of an outside consultant.

Lingering conflict is closely associated with declining membership. Conflict tends to cast a shadow across the activities and ethos

Figure 8.5. Relationship between Openness in Dealing with Conflict and High Vitality, by Percentage of Congregations Claiming High Vitality

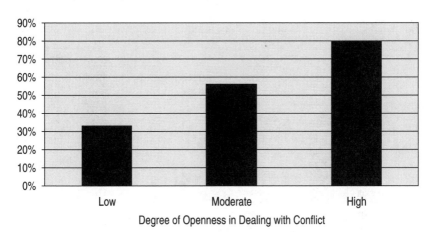

Degree of Openness in Dealing with Conflict

Source: Dudley and Roozen, *Faith Communities Today,* 61.

of the congregation as a whole, even the capacity to enlist volunteers. On the other hand, openness in dealing with conflict is closely associated with vitality (Figure 8.5). To recover a sense of mission and purpose, congregational leaders can encourage more open communication among members. According to the FACT study "capable leadership that enables openness in dealing with conflict can dramatically neutralize and perhaps even constructively use the energy of strong feelings that are typically present in bitter disagreements. Relatedly, congregations in which members' expectations and communal goals are clear are much more likely to deal openly with disagreements and conflicts" (Figure 8.6).[60]

"Indeed, openness in dealing with conflict does not imply a lack of standards or a loss of discipline. In fact, the opposite appears to be the case. Congregations that have unclear or implicit expectations for members are far more likely to experience higher levels

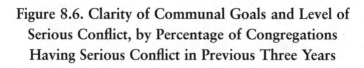

Figure 8.6. Clarity of Communal Goals and Level of Serious Conflict, by Percentage of Congregations Having Serious Conflict in Previous Three Years

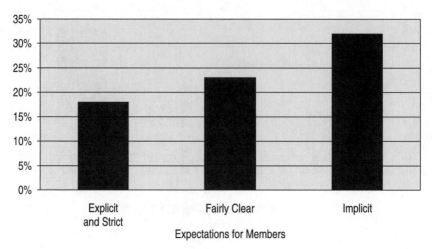

Source: Dudley and Roozen, *Faith Communities Today*, 62.

of conflict (Figure 8.7). Effective leadership in congregations is not simply a matter of openness in dealing with conflict, but helping them recognize and express their purpose in action."[61]

Finally, an interesting discovery in the FACT study, one that may have implications for those denominations and faith groups that provide theological education, is that "clergy with a seminary education are no more likely than other clergy to be in congregations that have a strong social justice orientation and are very much less likely to be in congregations that deal openly with conflict and disagreement."[62] This may require seminaries to review their educational curriculum and pastors to ask themselves some hard questions about their future ministry.

It is a maxim of sociological inquiry that education often tends to influence men and women toward middle-class, mainstream

Figure 8.7. Relationship between Clear Expectations and
Openness to Dealing with Conflict, by Percentage of
Congregations with High Openness in Dealing with Conflict

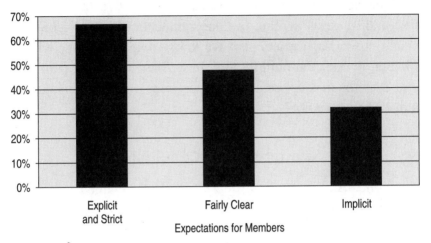

Source: Dudley and Roozen, *Faith Communities Today,* 63.

perspectives. In other words, the worldview of those with higher levels of education, particularly in Western culture, can be more accepting of and less challenging to the status quo. There are certainly exceptions to this theory, but there is evidence to suggest that those exceptions are just that.

Seminary training teaches women and men how to function in a religious social system. It prepares them to lead people in worship, service, and witness. How much our seminaries teach those preparing for ministry to manage conflict is unknown. How well our schools of theology prepare new pastors to be advocates for justice is also unknown. But these are important issues for denominations that require seminary training. If the world and local communities need pastors who are advocates for social justice, seminaries need to consider what they are teaching and what they are not. If conflict is present in our communities and our churches, seminarians need preparation to deal with it.

Men and women "of the cloth" need to ask themselves some hard questions. Do we avoid conflict? Are we advocates for social change and are we willing to take significant risks for economic, social, and racial justice? Are we knowledgeable about what is going on in our communities and do we have the courage to challenge systems that oppress and dehumanize our members, as well as those who are not?

Summary and Conclusion

Our biblical history points to great leadership called by God to lead God's people. Abraham, Moses, Deborah, David, and others are part of our Hebrew heritage. Paul, the disciples, and many others come from the period of the new covenant. God sent his only son, Jesus, to lead humanity toward community and shalom.

So many names of those we claim in our religious heritage could be and should be mentioned: Harriet Tubman, Sojourner Truth, Mary McLeod Bethune, Fannie Lou Homer, Richard Allen, Henry McNeal Turner, Marcus Garvey, and Martin Luther King Jr. are but a few.

Working with volunteers, building team approaches to problem solving and ministry, and utilizing nonprofit innovation for social and political outreach are necessary components of Black ministry. Education and preparation for the complexity of ministry are required. Social and political commitment and expressing one's views with courage and conviction are paramount. Finally, managing conflict and helping people take responsibility for individual and collective lives is essential as we push further into the new millennium. It is this kind of leadership that will be necessary as the Black Church looks to the future.

9

BLACK CHURCHES LOOK TO THE FUTURE

In this text we have shared information about African American congregational life as we know it. Our experience has been varied yet fruitful in understanding that unique and historic source of Black spirituality and religiosity. We have attempted to give an accurate picture of the African American religious setting based on current research. We have gone beyond the facts and tried to reveal some of the ways this current research can be understood, providing examples from local churches involving men and women as they practice their faith in the new millennium. We have suggested some of the ways these *facts* (national profile) and *faces* (local congregations) might be useful to you and others (*feelings*), especially in the *future*. It is our hope that this information will help those of us involved in ministry and mission to be more effective as we plan and execute our calling each and every day.

What we know about Black congregational life is important. The African American Church is located mostly in the southern and the north central parts of the United States. It is, generally speaking, an urban church. A majority of the Black churches have fewer than one hundred regularly participating adult members. Very few Black churches have been organized in the past ten years. Both the large and small that have multiple programs are growing in size.

The women and men who attend these local congregations are willing to travel more than fifteen minutes to be a part of them. Persons of all ages and stages of life are choosing to be active participants in the church. When comparing the general profile of these congregants to current census data we discovered that the congregations appear to be attracting representative percentages of college graduates and people sixty years of age and older. The two groups that are underrepresented are young people between the ages of eighteen and thirty-five and families whose total income falls below $20,000.

The pastors interviewed for this study reported that they felt their congregations could be described as being "spiritually vital and alive." They believed their members were deepening their relationships with God. They felt excited about the future. The men and women leading the African American congregations were themselves hopeful and enlivened.

The pastors reported that they preached with regularity on topics of God's love and care, personal spiritual growth, and practical advice for daily living. A majority of the pastoral leaders indicated that they used spirituals in their worship settings. They affirmed the use of sacred Scripture and the presence of the Holy Spirit in their worship and study life.

The local church provides an important nurturing function. Bible study, prayer groups, community services, and youth programs are all part of this internal community. They help children and adults to discover community and in many ways prepare them to provide community for individuals and families beyond their doors. And what many African American churches are providing for others is quite astonishing: youth programs, cash assistance to families and individuals, voter registration, food pantry and soup kitchens, counseling services, tutoring, prison ministry and more.

In fact, according to the larger national FACT survey among forty-one different denominational groups and faith communities, the historically Black churches are more involved in their communities than any other group.

The Black churches have many important resources — both soft (relational) and hard (countable). They have people, money, space, and facilities. They have a strong historical sense of philanthropy. The members choose to support their churches with their time, talents, and tithes. Because they choose to be faithful in the use of their resources, they are able to do the varied kinds of outreach described in chapter 6.

The Black Church has a rich heritage of strong and effective pastoral leadership. Our study discovered that many of the clergy who serve these churches are fairly well educated. They support involvement in civil rights and protest activities. They feel that their churches should express their views on social and political issues. Many don't believe that women should be pastors in a local church.

Some Implications of the Data from Congregational Survey Research

A major concern of studies in the field is to discover, examine, and share with the congregations ways in which the research could help. The goal is to assist them as they envision new possibilities and shape their future to be faithful and effective agents in the transformation of the lives of persons in our society. The data from the research has implications not only for the academic discipline, but also for every area of congregational life, including those areas not covered by the study. Indeed, the data raises new questions for exploration and examination. We wish to offer some additional reflections on our reading of the data. The observations we make are not intended to be definitive or exhaustive. From our experiences of relationship with pastors and congregations at different levels, we offer some comments for response.

Need for More Research

There is need for more research. The respondents in this study were largely pastors, assistant pastors, or senior lay leaders. It is important to gather the views and perspectives of members whose perceptions may be different from the pastors in terms of what's really going on. We have engaged some congregations and their leaders in a process of self-reflection and self-examination, using the instrument that we used in Project 2000. That resource is available from the office of the ITC Institute for Black Religious Life, 700 Martin Luther King Jr. Drive, S.W., Atlanta GA 30314. This approach brings persons other than pastors into assessing what is going on in the congregation. We would commend that instrument as one resource.

There is need for more ethnographic studies of congregations. Surveys with multiple-choice questions on a scale are extremely useful. Like ours, they provide profiles. More concentrated studies of individual congregations or clusters of congregations can yield data that will help us trace patterns and develop models of congregational life. We need to provide resources for congregations to engage in ongoing self-evaluation.

Congregational Self-Understanding and Ministry

What is the connection between the self-understanding of a congregation and its mission and ministry? Congregations have the capacity to affect their context through ways in which they organize themselves and engage that context. Conversely the environment in which they find themselves affects and shapes the lives of congregations. Where congregations are in touch with their own identity and community context, they are better able to define their purpose and involve their people in meaningful ministry. As we engage in fulfilling our mission as a congregation, we need to consider our place in our community and the influence we are having on its life. What are the entry points for the gospel into the life of the community for which we are concerned? How does the faith we profess relate to concrete conditions of persons in our community?

Intergenerational Ministry

How seriously do congregations take ministry not only to the different generations, but also between the generations? What are resources for developing effective programs in this area? In what ways will such programs benefit the whole congregation and further and promote an understanding of its mission?

Congregations must seek to confront the tensions that exist between the generations, as they seek to bring together all persons within the household of faith. They must explore creative ways to foster a sense of family so that all persons grow in love for one another and affirm community within the congregation.

Youth Ministry

Pastors surveyed reported that youth programs were offered in 92 percent of their congregations. Are youth permitted and encouraged to freely express their ideas? How well does your congregation understand the youth who are searching and exhibit an interest in the church? Are the leaders who are recruited for youth programs serious about working with and serving youth on youth's terms?

Attendance and Participation in Congregational Life

The percentage of regularly participating adults and typical church attendance is significantly lower than the numbers on the church rolls. This, we believe, raises questions about the meaning of membership and the educational task of enabling persons to grow in their faith development. What educational programs address this concern in your congregation?

Tithing and Financial Support

Nearly all pastors reported that at least some of their members tithe (95 percent). Pastors were also asked about the percentage of members who tithe in their congregation. The average is about 45 percent. The overall financial health of the congregations interviewed appears to be getting stronger. It seems to suggest that more congregations need to consider tithing as a way not only to fiscal vitality, but also to a deepened commitment of members.

Conflict in Congregational Life

Conflicts reported in congregations are generally around worship and finances. Conflict can negatively impact member growth, but where earnest efforts are made to address conflict, the vitality of congregational life is increased both in spirituality and numbers. Additionally, the connection between knowledge of and commitment to heritage and the increased potential for vitality and growth suggests an area for sustained educational efforts. Perhaps you need to have conversations in your congregation to discover the sources of conflict and how successful they are being dealt with. Does conflict create factions and cause rifts that cannot be mended in your congregation? What resources are available to you and do you need to seek to restore those areas of brokenness in your congregational life?

Interfaith and Ecumenical Activities

The data indicates that 60 percent of Black congregations are involved in interfaith activities with white congregations. There is no indication, however, of the nature of those activities. This is an area where opportunities exist for the development of partnerships and alliances in particular geographic contexts to address the needs of persons. Much anecdotal evidence suggests that there are activities and relationships, but the challenge invites congregations to discover what needs to be done and who is doing what. We need to choose those partnerships we wish to form, identify resources that are available, and commit ourselves to ministries that express concern for the common welfare of persons. There is an opportunity for interfaith cooperation that should be vigorously pursued.

Evaluating Congregational Life

Congregations have as their fundamental task to invite and receive people as they are, whoever they are, to relate them to God, to nurture and develop them as disciples, and to send them out into communities to make those communities more loving and just. Lyle Schaller offers sage comment for congregations seeking to discover their health. Those who seek "to identify the marks of a healthy church focus on such words as love, servanthood, compassion, humility, faithfulness, worship, forgiveness, obedience, justice, prayer, community, teaching and martyrdom."[63]

We remind readers that what we have provided in this book is a series of profiles of African American congregations in their denominational character. We have sought to draw your attention to similarities and differences between individual denominations and against the national profile. You know what the reality is in your congregation or congregations that you know. We are not suggesting that the profiles are definitive or exhaustive of the realities in local congregations. They are, however, illustrative and offer glimpses into those realities.

We invite you to check the data against what you know in your context. How do you compare or in what areas is your congregation different? What do you perceive as challenges? We encourage you not only to engage in self-evaluation, but also to exercise your creative imagination and think of new and different possibilities for your congregational life in all its varied dimensions. We challenge you, after serious and critical examination of your own congregation's life, to find ways into a future that you envision and to which you will be committed.

The following general questions may be used to evoke answers about strengths or challenges:

- How do you understand your *mission* (purpose) as people of God and how faithful and obedient are you to that mission?

- What is the level of *participation* of the total membership? Is there a place where persons have a sense of *belonging* and involvement in the community, where their gifts are celebrated and used, and they are affirmed?

- How does the *leadership* assist in sharing in the responsibility for fulfilling the congregation's mission as people of God?

Congregations, like persons, need a checkup from time to time to ensure their proper functioning. We hope that our book is one resource that can help you and your congregation engage in that necessary checkup that can reveal new and different ways of enhancing your life together.

The Black Church and Tensions in Public Involvement

Black churches have a new challenge in response to government proposals to make funding available to support work that churches have already been doing with limited resources. Many Black churches and pastors have responded to identified needs and hurts of people in their communities by delivering a variety of social services. But the complexities of the situations demand approaches and skills for which most Black pastors need preparation and training. There needs to be an affirmation of the interrelationship between social, political, and economic life. The Church must broaden its focus beyond traditional political activism and address the fact that the current needs of the Black community are largely economic.

There is a hesitancy on the part of Black Church leaders to be involved with government-funded programs. The fears that some pastors have expressed relate to their anxiety about financial scrutiny. These fears can be addressed as clergy learn how to establish Community Development Corporations (CDCs) and thus avoid commingling of funds. More formal training is called for in economic and community development ministries, including training in forming partnerships with civic agencies for the common welfare of persons.

The availability of funding to do what the Black Church seeks to do for the disadvantaged continues to create tensions for Black Church leadership. The tensions include:

1. Should we continue our work with limited resources or accept the resources of "Big Brother" with all the associated constraints and scrutiny?

2. Are we willing to accept the criticism of others in the Black community who accuse us of "selling out"?

3. Are we willing to compromise in theological, political, and social ideology?

4. Are we able to extract sufficient support from our membership or should we also seek assistance from philanthropic foundations or partner with other unlikely groups (e.g., government agencies, theologically different churches and institutions, etc.).

In order to avail themselves of opportunities provided by the currently popular faith-based initiatives, Black churches and pastors require greater preparation to navigate the systems to the benefit of the deserving. There are many pastors who have led congregations into ministry that makes a difference in their communities. Perhaps those pastors can be resources for others who are interested but are uninformed and hesitant. It will mean willingness on the part of those who have the knowledge to share that knowledge. Ways and models need to be found and shared to increase the number of pastors who are empowered through training to make full use of opportunities presented.

Being Spiritually Alive

Vital congregations have a clear sense of purpose and explicit member expectations that are strictly enforced. They have a more positive assessment about the future. There is a distinct connection between clarity of purpose and the quality and quantity of financial support.

Spiritually vital congregations comprise groups in which persons have a sense of who they are, regularly explore the meaning of their faith, and mutually support one another. They find and create places for persons to discover and use their gifts and skills to assist the congregation in fulfilling its mission. Through the disciplines of prayer and Bible study in private and public worship, persons experience relationship with God. Spiritually vital congregations enable persons in a variety of ways to find and make connections between their faith and daily life.

Belonging and Finding Meaning in Congregational Life

Persons are looking for a place to belong and experience a sense of community. They are searching for meaning in life and meaningful relationships. They are also looking for an opportunity to share their gifts and talents in satisfying and worthy engagements. As they turn to the congregation as a source of satisfaction for these longings in their souls, they need to be lovingly received, related to God, nurtured, and prepared to engage in labor that brings the reign of God nearer in everyday life. The congregation is a place to belong in relationship, not only with one another, but also and most importantly with God.

A New Frontier upon Us

Within the last two decades a new frontier has broken upon our world: the Information Age. There is a whole new vocabulary, a new set of techniques, and new technologies. We are in the age of the "instant," where our insatiable cravings are satisfied — right now. Click a mouse, make some choices, give some commands, and, behold, the information is available. If you can figure out how that works, you are truly "wired." The pace of change is faster than it has ever been in human history. Breakthroughs in communications, travel, machinery, and medicine have all revolutionized the ways in which we think, live, and do ministry. In this age of sophistication are we in the Church still in the horse and buggy days? Can the Church respond quickly and intelligibly in an increasingly complex world?

Every congregation that seeks to fulfill its mission announces that the Lord is present amid the struggles of human beings for peace and justice, and that the last word is with God. Through our involvement in God's mission in the world, we must lead persons to recognize the relation between faith and human existence, between faith and social reality, between the reign of God and the building up of the world. The Church is inescapably bound up with the human family. It is impossible to reject the pressure of the contemporary world and this new millennium into which we have entered. We cannot run away from the world of facts and be altogether indifferent and unresponsive. The world cannot afford such a Church nor a community such a congregation. The work of every congregation is part of the struggle of humankind in which we are called to participate as co-laborers with God.

We serve a living God who challenges us out of our complacency and our tendency to cling to the structures we build and the principles and systems we employ. Structures become arthritic and ultimately dehumanizing. Today's structures, reflecting faithfulness and obedience now, may be obsolete tomorrow. So we must continue to labor against the idolatry of absolutizing our systems and structures — and even our surveys. There is much in congregational life that cannot be empirically tested, but our hope is that our book has provided some insights for all who seek to deepen their understanding of congregational life.

To Be the Word of Hope

The Church is called to proclaim constantly a word of hope in the midst of hopelessness, to infuse life with meaning, and to maintain a vision of hope. John was imprisoned for engaging in the prophetic role, for "telling it like it is" (Luke 13:18–21). John sent his disciples to ask Jesus, in effect, "Is the kingdom coming?" Jesus replies, "Go and tell John what you have seen and heard, the blind receive their sight, the lame walk, the lepers are cleansed, the deaf hear, the dead are raised, the poor have the good news brought to them. And blessed is he who takes no offense at me" (Luke 7:19–23). That's the Gospel!

Appendix

RESEARCH METHODOLOGY

ITC/FaithFactor Project 2000 is a research and educational program of ITC/FaithFactor, a faith-based community revitalization initiative of the Interdenominational Theological Center. ITC, located in Atlanta, Georgia, contracted with The Gallup Organization to assist with the ITC's study of Black congregational life.

The ITC is a Christian, ecumenical, graduate professional school of theology. Six historically African American denominational bodies are part of the ITC consortium — Morehouse School of Religion (Baptist), Gammon Theological Seminary (United Methodist), Turner Theological Seminary (African Methodist Episcopal), Phillips School of Theology (Christian Methodist Episcopal), Johnson C. Smith Theological Seminary (Presbyterian U.S.A.), and Charles H. Mason Seminary (Church of God in Christ).

During the spring of 2000, Gallup began interviewing pastors of Black and predominately Black congregations across the nation in order to gain a clear and comprehensive understanding of their communities of faith. Included in this survey of nearly two thousand pastors and senior lay leaders were questions on the focus of their sermons, community service, challenges and disputes within the congregation, the financial health of the churches, and background characteristics of pastors and their congregations.

In order to obtain data from a cross-section of clergy with predominately Black congregations, telephone interviews were conducted with pastors of seven denominations — Baptist, Church of God in Christ (COGIC), African Methodist Episcopal (AME), Christian Methodist Episcopal (CME), African Methodist Episcopal Zion (AMEZ), Black United Methodist, and Black Presbyterian (U.S.A.).

A total of 1,863 pastors or senior lay leaders were surveyed. The telephone interviews averaged sixteen minutes in length.

The following Figure A.1 indicates the total number of completed interviews by quota group and the margin of error associated with each.

Figure A.1. Interviews among Black Protestant Groups

	Total Number of Interviews	Margin of Error +/- Points
Total	1863	2.3%
Baptist	502	4.4%
COGIC	503	4.4%
AME	257	6.1%
CME	295	5.7%
AMEZ	110	9.0%
UMC	95	10.1%
Presbyterian	101	9.8%

A sample for this survey was produced by the Interdenominational Theological Center from lists of congregations throughout the nation. The primary list was provided by Tri-Media.

Screening for this survey included an initial question, which attempted to gain the cooperation of the pastor. If the pastor was not available, Gallup interviewed either the church's assistant or a senior lay leader. Of the 1,863 total of interviews, 1,482 (80 percent) were conducted with the pastor while 381 (20 percent) were conducted with the senior lay leader or assistant pastor.

The survey data was weighted to reflect the latest available estimates of the number of congregations within each denomination interviewed. This weighing step was designed to correct the disproportional size of the denominations introduced by setting interview quotas. Estimates were obtained from the Tri-Media list and other lists of churches throughout the United States.

NOTES

1. Michael I. N. Dash, Jonathan Jackson, and Stephen C. Rasor, *Hidden Wholeness: An African American Spirituality for Individuals and Communities* (Cleveland: Pilgrim Press, 1997), vii.

2. Michael I. N. Dash, Stephen C. Rasor, and Christine D. Chapman, *ITC/FaithFactor Project 2000 Study of Black Churches* (Atlanta: Interdenominational Theological Center, 2001).

3. C. Eric Lincoln and Lawrence H. Mamiya, *The Black Church in the African American Experience* (Durham, N.C.: Duke University Press, 1990), 2.

4. Ibid., 344–45.

5. Jewelle Taylor Gibbs, ed., *Young, Black, and Male in America: An Endangered Species* (Dover, Mass.: Auburn House, 1988).

6. Andrew Billingsley, *Mighty Like a River: The Black Church and Social Reform* (New York: Oxford University Press, 1999), 102.

7. Ibid., 91.

8. The phenomenon of Black megachurches was an ancillary part of our study of Black congregational life. A report on the current state of those churches is found in Tamelyn Tucker-Worgs, "Get on Board Little Children, There's Room for Many More: The Black Megachurch Phenomenon," *Journal of the Interdenominational Theological Center* 29, nos. 1–2 (Fall 2001–Spring 2002): 177–203.

9. Carl S. Dudley and David A. Roozen, *Faith Communities Today: A Report on Religion in the United States Today* (Hartford, Conn.: Hartford Institute for Religion Research, Hartford Seminary, 2001), 20–24.

10. Ibid., 16.

11. Ibid., 17.

12. L. Anderson, *Dying for Change* (Minneapolis: Bethany House, 1990), 237.

13. Valentino Lassiter, *Martin Luther King in the African American Preaching Tradition* (Cleveland: Pilgrim Press, 2001), 7.

14. Melva Wilson Costen, "African-American Worship: Faith Looking Forward," *Journal of the Interdenominational Theological Center* 27, nos. 1–2 (Fall 1999–Spring 2000), 1.

15. William B. McClain, "What Is Authentic Black Worship?" in *Experiences, Struggles, and Hopes of the Black Church*, ed. James S. Gadsen (Nashville: Discipleship Resources–Tidings, 1975), 70.

16. Dudley and Roozen, *Faith Communities Today,* 29.

17. Ibid., 37.

18. Lincoln and Mamiya, *The Black Church in the African American Experience,* 386.

19. Vincent L. Wimbush, "The Bible and African Americans: An Outline of an Interpretive History," in *Stony the Road We Trod: African American Biblical Interpretation,* ed. Cain Hope Felder (Minneapolis: Fortress Press, 1991), 83.

20. Dash, Jackson, and Rasor, *Hidden Wholeness,* 26–27.

21. Dudley and Roozen, *Faith Communities Today,* 43.

22. Ibid., 49.

23. Lincoln and Mamiya, *The Black Church in the African American Experience,* 242.

24. Cecil Williams and Rebecca Laird, *No Hiding Place: Empowerment and Recovery for Our Troubled Communities* (New York: HarperCollins, 1992).

25. Lea E. Williams, *Servants of the People: The 1960s Legacy of African American Leadership* (New York: St. Martin's Press, 1996).

26. Ronald E. Nored, Sr., *Reweaving the Fabric: How Congregations and Communities Can Come Together to Build Their Neighborhoods* (Montgomery, Ala.: Black Belt Press, 1999), 12.

27. James A. Forbes Jr., "Social Transformation," in *Living with Apocalypse: Spiritual Resources for Social Compassion,* ed. Tilden Edwards (San Francisco: Harper and Row Publishers, 1984), 41.

28. Billingsley, *Mighty like a River.*

29. *A Study on Financing African-American Churches: National Survey on Church Giving* (Atlanta: Institute of Church Administration and Management, 1997).

30. Ibid.

31. Dudley and Roozen, *Faith Communities Today.*

32. Nancy T. Ammerman et al., *Studying Congregations: A New Handbook* (Nashville: Abingdon Press, 1998), 132.

33. Dudley and Roozen, *Faith Communities Today*, 32.

34. Dash, Rasor, and Chapman, *ITC/FaithFactor Project 2000 Study of Black Churches.*

35. *A Study on Financing African-American Churches.*

36. Dudley and Roozen, *Faith Communities Today*, 54.

37. Ibid., 55.

38. Kennon L. Callahan, *Building for Effective Mission: A Complete Guide for Congregations on Bricks and Mortar Issues* (San Francisco: HarperSanFrancisco, 1995), 51–52.

39. See Tucker-Worgs, "Get on Board Little Children, There's Room for Many More," 177–203.

40. K. Sue Jewell, *The Survival of the Black Family: The Institutional Impact of U.S. Social Policy* (New York: Praeger, 1988), 36.

41. Andrew H. Billingsley and Jeanne M. Giovannoni, *Children of the Storm: Black Children and American Child Welfare* (New York: Harcourt, Brace, Jovanovich, 1972), 46.

42. Lincoln and Mamiya, *The Black Church in the African American Experience*, 242.

43. Jewell, *The Survival of the Black Family*, 41.

44. Ibid., 29.

45. John S. Mbiti, *African Religion and Philosophy* (Nairobi, Kenya: Heinemann, 1996), 108.

46. Ibid., 108–9.

47. Wade Clark Roof and William McKinney, *American Mainline Religion* (New Brunswick, N.J.: Rutgers University Press, 1987), 91.

48. Lincoln and Mamiya, *The Black Church in the African American Experience*, 242.

49. Jewell, *The Survival of the Black Family*, 27–29.

50. Robert Staples, *Introduction to Black Sociology* (New York: McGraw-Hill, 1976), 76.

51. Ibid.

52. James Moffatt, *A Critical and Exegetical Commentary of the Epistle to the Hebrews* (Edinburgh: T. & T. Clark, 1957), 62.

53. Lyle E. Schaller, *Innovations in Ministry into the Twenty-first Century* (Nashville: Abingdon, 1998), 59.

54. John P. Kotter, "What Leaders Really Do," *Harvard Business Review* (December 2001): 85.

55. Peter Drucker, "What Business Can Learn from Nonprofits," *Harvard Business Review* (July–August 1989).

56. Dudley and Roozen, *Faith Communities Today,* 21.

57. Kotter, "What Leaders Really Do," 85.

58. Cheryl Townsend Gilkes, *"If It Wasn't for Women—" Black Women's Experience and Womanist Culture in Church and Community* (Maryknoll, N.Y.: Orbis Books, 2001), 7.

59. Delores C. Carpenter, *A Time for Honor: A Portrait of African American Clergywomen* (St. Louis: Chalice Press, 2001).

60. Dudley and Roozen, *Faith Communities Today,* 62.

61. Ibid., 63.

62. Ibid., 66.

63. Lyle E. Schaller, "Marks of a Healthy Church," *The Parish Paper of the Yokefellow Institute,* Fall 1983.

SELECTED BIBLIOGRAPHY

Ammerman, Nancy Tatom, Jackson Carroll, and Carl Dudley. *Studying Congregations: A New Handbook.* Nashville: Abingdon Press, 1998.

Ammerman, Nancy Tatom, with Arthur Farnsley II. *Congregation and Community.* New Brunswick, N.J.: Rutgers University Press, 1997.

Anderson, Terry D. *Transforming Leadership: New Skills for an Extraordinary Future.* Amherst, Mass.: Human Resource Development Press, 1992.

Becker, Penny Edgell. *Congregations in Conflict: Cultural Model of Local Religious Life.* New York: Cambridge University Press, 1999.

Billingsley, Andrew. *Mighty like a River: The Black Church and Social Reform.* New York: Oxford University Press, 1999.

Billingsley, Andrew, and Jeanne Giovannoni, *Children Of the Storm.* New York: Harcourt, Brace and Jovanovich, 1972.

Callahan, Kennon R. *A New Beginning for Pastors and Congregations: Building an Excellent Match on Your Shared Strengths.* San Francisco: Jossey-Bass, 1999.

Carpenter, Delores C. *A Time for Honor: A Portrait of African American Clergywomen.* St. Louis: Chalice Press, 2001.

Carroll, Jackson W. *Mainline to the Future: Congregations for the Twenty-first Century.* Louisville: Westminster John Knox Press, 2000.

Dudley, Carl S., and Nancy T. Ammerman. *Congregations in Transition: A Guide for Analyzing, Assessing, and Adapting to Changing Communities.* San Francisco: Jossey-Bass, 2002.

Dudley, Carl S., and David A. Roozen, *Faith Communities Today: A Report on Religion in the United States Today.* Hartford, Conn.: Hartford Institute for Research, Hartford Seminary, 2001.

Gallup, George, Jr., and D. Michael Lindsay. *Surveying the Religious Landscape: Trends in U.S. Beliefs.* Harrisburg, Pa.: Morehouse Publishing, 1999.

Gilkes, Cheryl Townsend. *"If It Wasn't for Women—" Black Women's Experience and Womanist Culture in Church and Community.* Maryknoll, N.Y.: Orbis Books, 2001.

Harris, James H. *Black Ministers and Laity in the Urban Church: An Analysis of Political and Social Expectations.* Lanham, Md.: University Press of America, 1987.

Herrington, Jim, Mike Bonem, and James H. Furr. *Leading Congregational Change: A Practical Guide for the Transformational Journey.* San Francisco: Jossey-Bass, 2000.

Jewell, K. Sue. *Survival of the Black Family: The Institutional Impact of U.S. Social Policy.* New York: Praeger, 1988.

Job, Reuben P. *Spiritual Life in the Congregation: A Guide for Retreats.* Nashville: Upper Room Books, 1997.

Johnson, Douglas W. *Empowering Lay Volunteers.* Creative Leadership Series. Nashville: Abingdon, 1991.

Lassiter, Valentino. *Martin Luther King in the African American Preaching Tradition.* Cleveland: Pilgrim Press, 2001

Lincoln, C. Eric, and Lawrence H. Mamiya. *The Black Church in the African American Experience.* Durham, N.C.: Duke University Press, 1990.

Mbiti, John S. *African Religion and Philosophy,* Nairobi, Kenya: Heinemann, 1996.

———. *Concepts of God in Africa.* New York: Praeger, 1970.

McKenzie, Vashti M. *Not without a Struggle: Leadership Development for African American Women in Ministry.* Cleveland: United Church Press, 1996.

Mead, Loren B. *Transforming Congregations for the Future.* New York: Alban Institute, 1994.

Miller, Donald E. *Reinventing American Protestantism: Christianity in the New Millennium.* Berkeley: University of California Press, 1999.

Nessan, Craig L. *Beyond Maintenance to Mission: A Theology of the Congregation.* Minneapolis: Fortress Press, 1999.

Olson, Mark A. *Moving beyond Church Growth: An Alternative Vision for Congregations.* Minneapolis: Fortress Press, 2000.

Oswald, Robert M., and Robert E. Friedrich. *Discerning Your Congregation's Future: A Strategic and Spiritual Approach.* New York: Alban Institute, 1990.

Rabey, Steve. *In Search of Authentic Faith: How Emerging Generations Are Transforming the Church*. Colorado Springs, Colo.: Waterbrook Press, 2001.

Roof, Wade Clark, and William McKinney, *American Mainline Religion*. New Brunswick, N.J.: Rutgers University Press, 1987.

Schaller, Lyle E. *Innovations in Ministry: Models for the Twenty-first Century*. Nashville: Abingdon, 1994.

Staples, Robert, *Introduction to Black Sociology*. New York: McGraw-Hill, 1976.

Stewart, Carlyle Fielding, III. *The Empowerment Church: Speaking a New Language for Church Growth*. Nashville: Abingdon, 2001.

A Study on Financing African-American Churches — National Survey on Church Giving. Atlanta: Institute of Church Administration and Management, 1997.

Thompson, George B., Jr. *How to Get Along with Your Church: Creating Cultural Capital for Doing Ministry*. Cleveland: Pilgrim Press, 2001.

Wallis, Jim. *Faith Works: Lessons from an Activist Preacher*. New York: Random House, 2000.

Wilkes, Paul. *Excellent Protestant Congregations: The Guide to Best Places and Practices*. Louisville: Westminster John Knox Press, 2000.

Williams, Lea E. *Servants of the People: The 1960s Legacy of African American Leadership*. New York: St. Martin's Press, 1996.

INDEX

Page references in *bold italics* indicate figures.